A WORK LIFE WORTH LIVING

YOUR GUIDE TO CREATING A MEANINGFUL CAREER

JEFFREY R. WESTPHAL

Foreword by Joseph Jaworski, best-selling author of
Synchronicity: The Inner Path of Leadership

RIVER GROVE
BOOKS

"An evergreen book exploring humanity's most enduring question: 'What gives life meaning?' And in an age where work occupies so much of our existence, we must also ask 'What gives *work* meaning?' As generative AI increasingly takes over analytical intelligence, Jeff reminds us of Aristotle's deeper insight that wisdom—the art of a fully lived life—is the true human achievement. A book for everyone who chooses to live deliberately."

—ISAAC GETZ, best-selling coauthor of *Freedom, Inc.* and *The Caring Company*

"For anyone seeking to understand the deeper dimensions of leadership, personal growth, and the human side of business, Jeff's story is an invaluable resource. This book is not merely a chronicle of business success; it is a reflection on what it means to live a meaningful life, both in the workplace and beyond."

—DON HUIZENGA, former CEO, Kurdziel Industries; former president, American Foundry Society; board member, EQI, an Atlas Holdings company

"Jeff's book shows the world of work as a place where profound personal growth can happen. It captures this personal development in the story of one man's exploration of what a person can do with their life and how they can learn from *their* experiences. It points to how helpful it is to have wise mentors, the courage to seek them out, and the willingness to engage deeply with their questions."

—LANI MORRIS, cofounder, Map of Meaning International; coauthor of *The Map of Meaningful Work*

"This was an absolute joy to read. As a parent of two young adults, I want this book for *them*. Jeff speaks to their generation honestly, earnestly, and understandingly, meeting them where they are and inviting them in through stories and epiphanies. It's that intimate, old-school-style mentoring this generation has largely missed. The book uses the voice of the contemporary *Tuesdays with Morrie*—only instead of end of life, it's the start of a more meaningful work life."

—ED WALLACE, author of *Business Relationships That Last* and *The Relationship Engine*

"It's easy to dismiss things like mindset and meaning as a little touchy-feely, but these are virtues that matter in the business world. I learned this by watching the way Jeff led Vertex for more than twenty years. A significant part of our lives is spent at work, so why not make that time meaningful? When you find purpose in what you do for a living, your life improves in ways that can't be measured and your momentum becomes unstoppable."

—ERIK RUDA, CEO, Rize Technologies

"Jeff Westphal demystifies one of the greatest challenges of the modern era: how to find meaning in our professional lives without sacrificing success. Jeff doesn't just theorize from the CEO suite; he shares a vulnerable, hard-won road map for anyone who suspects there is 'something more' to work than a paycheck."

—DAVID G. HENKIN, tech executive; award-winning coauthor of *Fixing Work*

"Working for fifteen years in an environment shaped by Jeff's leadership taught me that meaning at work comes from trust, encouragement, and the freedom to take ownership of both my work and growth. That culture shaped how I approached my career, showing me that purpose and performance are not opposites. *A Work Life Worth Living* is a gift to the next generation of seekers looking to grow, lead, and bring others with them."

—DR. JOHN H. WILSON, professor,
Close School of Entrepreneurship, Drexel University

Published by River Grove Books
Austin, TX
www.rivergrovebooks.com

Distributed by River Grove Books

Design and composition by Greenleaf Book Group
Cover design by Greenleaf Book Group
Cover images used under license from ©Adobestock.com

Publisher's Cataloging-in-Publication data is available.

Paperback ISBN: 979-8-90052-057-5

Hardcover: 979-8-90052-067-4

eBook ISBN: 979-8-90052-058-2

First Edition

Praise for *A Work Life Worth Living*

"Jeff Westphal doesn't preach from the mountaintop. He writes from the wreckage—failed products, a 3-out-of-7 trust score, rehab at fifty, and more. His honesty about what he got wrong is precisely what makes his insights about meaning, mentorship, and listening land so hard."

—**DANIEL H. PINK,** #1 *New York Times* best-selling author of *The Power of Regret* and *Drive*

"*A Work Life Worth Living* is a road map for working and living; a must-read for anyone under forty!"

—**DAN RATHER,** legendary journalist; author of *What Unites Us*

"Jeff Westphal could have written the book his resume would suggest: a multibillion-dollar success story with lessons attached. Instead, he wrote something far more rare and far more valuable: the truth, generously told, with enough hard-won scar tissue to earn your trust. This book doesn't just tell you that meaningful work is possible. It shows you, with uncommon candor, what it costs—and what it's worth. In an age of artificial intelligence, that's a genuinely human achievement."

—**KATE O'NEILL,** the "Tech Humanist"; CEO, KO Insights; author of *What Matters Next*

"Jeff Westphal reframes work not as something we endure but as an expression of who we truly are. Whatever road you are on, Jeff helps you to transform 'work' from a four-letter word to the actualization of your deepest aspirations."

—JAY COEN GILBERT,
cofounder, AND1 and B Lab

"As more people seek meaning, fulfillment, and personal impact in their work lives beyond simply making money, this practical guide offers them valuable steps on how to achieve greater goals."

—SIR RONALD COHEN, cofounder, Apax Partners;
cofounder and president, GSG Impact; author of *Impact*

"A Work Life Worth Living is a powerful testimony of personal growth and a valuable choose-your-own-adventure treasure map for everyone who dares to create a work life that fills their soul—not just their bank account."

—DR. STACY FEINER, psychologist;
entrepreneur; coauthor of *The Sixth Level*

"Jeff Westphal has written a raw, honest, compelling, and inspiring book. *A Work Life Worth Living* is brutally authentic, elegantly clear, and quietly profound—a personal reckoning that becomes a generous guide for anyone who suspects there must be more to a career than achievement, momentum, or survival. Wise, humane, and deeply relatable for anyone trying to build a work life that actually means something."

—MATT TYRNAUER, director;
producer; writer; editor-at-large, *Vanity Fair*

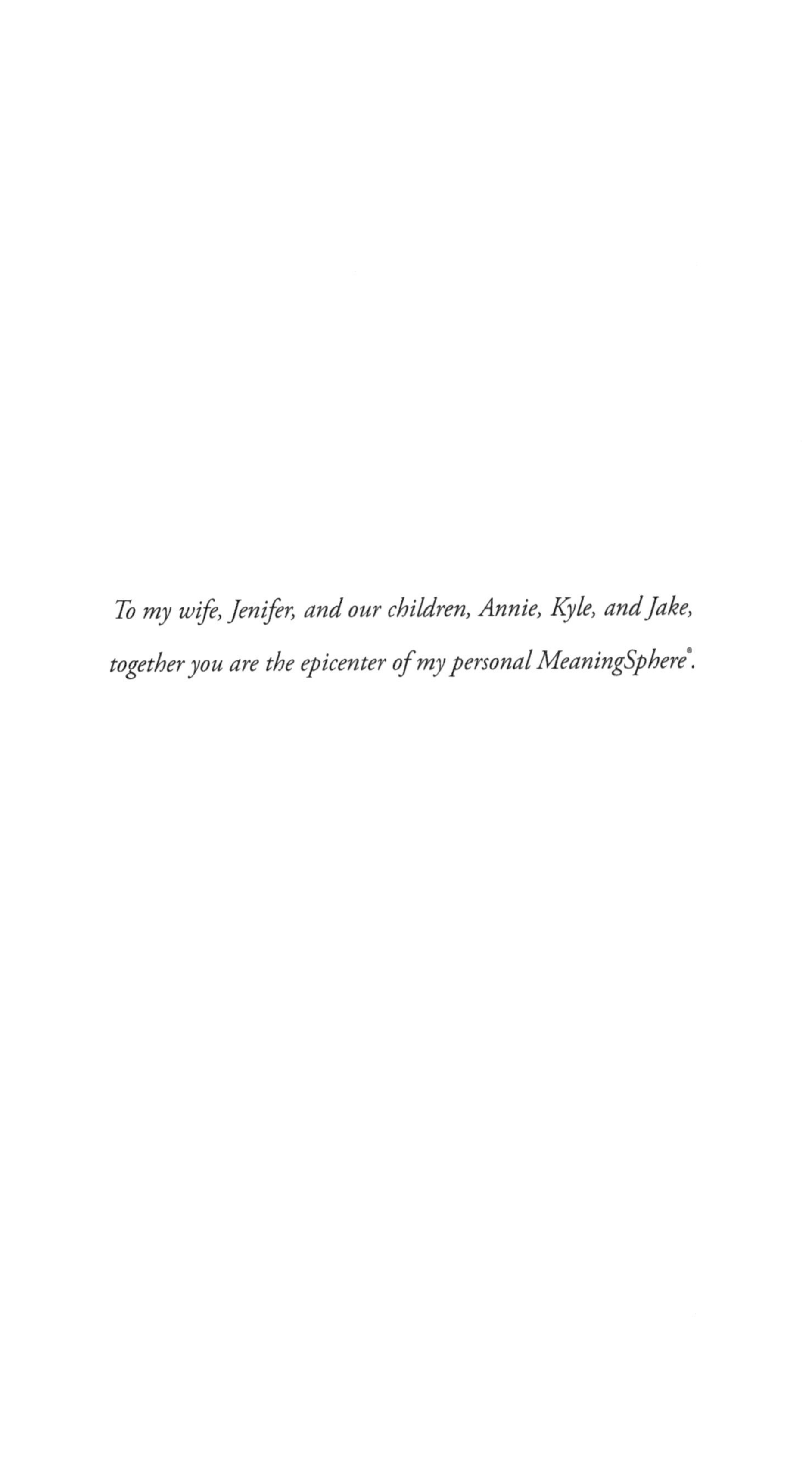

To my wife, Jenifer, and our children, Annie, Kyle, and Jake,

together you are the epicenter of my personal MeaningSphere®.

CONTENTS

PART II: UNDERSTANDING

PART III: ACTING

Author photograph by Christine M. Keeley

ABOUT JEFF WESTPHAL

In the mid-1990s, Jeff Westphal took over his father's upstart sales tax software business and, over the next two decades, built it into a dominant industry leader with nearly one thousand employees and over $300 million in annual revenue. Under Jeff's leadership, Vertex became an essential cog in the commerce machine, relied upon by more than ten thousand of the largest companies in the world.

In July of 2020, after Jeff's retirement as CEO in 2017, Vertex went public on the NASDAQ stock exchange and is now valued in the billions. It is a great American success story—but telling that story is not the purpose of this book.

Behind this success story is another, more complex story of how a leader found, then lost and found again, meaning in his life and work—and how, by helping his employees create meaning in work as seemingly meaningless as sales tax software, he helped his company survive challenges and thrive.

Today, Jeff is a seasoned executive, entrepreneur, philanthropist, corporate culture enthusiast, and conservationist. In addition to leading Vertex for two decades, he has founded two new ventures—MeaningSphere® and Mosaic™—as he continues to give back and encourage others to create meaning in their learning and working lives.

A Work Life Worth Living is not a business book focused on tales of success and fame. Instead, it shares an honest process of self-discovery and growth from a business leader who has come full circle to what matters most in a work life.

Jeff's story shows that even mundane work does not have to be drudgery and that finding greater meaning in one's work often leads to a more fulfilling life and career. It is honest and inspirational. It is, at times, profound, and it is also full of simple common sense. Its purpose is to support you on the path toward greater self-understanding and growth. To learn more, visit jeffwestphal.org and meaningsphere.com.

FOREWORD

by Joseph Jaworski

Joseph Jaworski is the critically acclaimed author of *Synchronicity: The Inner Path of Leadership* and *Source: The Inner Path of Knowledge Creation*, as well as coauthor of *Presence: Human Purpose and the Field of the Future*. For nearly five decades, Joseph has worked with leaders around the world to cultivate organizations grounded in shared purpose and collective intelligence. He brings to this foreword not only deep experience in leadership and transformation, but also a close personal and professional relationship with Jeff, shaped through years of shared inquiry and collaboration.

Jeff Westphal is one of my closest and most trusted friends. What I respect most about him is not only what he has built, but who he has become through the building of it. His clarity of purpose, his authenticity, and his deep commitment to serving humankind did not arrive easily or by accident. They were shaped through real struggle, real questions, and real moments of reckoning that formed the wisdom he now shares with you.

I know firsthand the courage it has taken for Jeff to face his own fears, follow his own calling, and stay true to what matters most. So, I stand on solid ground when I share what I have written here and why it is important for you to read this book.

This book is a companion to you, not an instruction manual. It is for those of us like me when I was twenty-seven, mostly clueless, but hungry to learn.

Each of us is born with a destiny, a purpose in life. The way to find fulfillment and happiness is to discover that purpose . . . that true purpose . . . not one that simply meets the expectations of others.

This book will help you make that discovery.

Throughout these pages, Jeff speaks directly to us about our own purpose. Early on, he tells the story of his first mentor, Jim Patton, who urged Jeff to clarify his own purpose as a pathway to personal fulfillment.

It is an easy read. Jeff's stories are simple but powerful, because the truths behind them are universal. This book is not written from the mountaintop. It is written from the road; the same one you are on.

Life itself follows a universal pattern of inner growth described in this book: departure, crossing the threshold to confront our fears, discovering meaning, and bringing back wisdom to our ordinary world. The lesson is that each of us has the potential for heroic self-discovery.

This book becomes a map for navigating that journey toward personal transformation, inviting you to follow your own authentic path, embrace challenges, and realize your potential for a richer, more meaningful life in service to your community.

Jeff's own life journey led him to found MeaningSphere, a valuable resource created to support people like you in bringing more meaning into your work and your life. Joining this community is a genuine learning opportunity grounded in decades of research, guided by experienced practitioners.

If you dream of living a life of adventure and meaning, read this book. It is a true gem.

With respect,

JOSEPH JAWORSKI

Wimberley, Texas

WHY READ THIS BOOK?

A growing list of blue-chip research studies conclude that most people want their work lives to matter but are unfulfilled in their careers. This is true of people working in all kinds of jobs, from the entry level to the C-suite.

Many of us work to meet our basic needs but don't find that our work gives us any sense of deep personal satisfaction. Others don't even believe that their work *could* be personally fulfilling.

That's what I believed when I first entered the working world four decades ago. I wound up in a job I did well in but with no sense of meaning beyond the satisfaction of checking off a seemingly endless to-do list.

That's how it was—but I'm living proof it doesn't have to be that way. Thanks to the journey this book describes, I found deep personal meaning in the strangest of all places—corporate sales tax software. Not exactly the Peace Corps, but that is precisely the point. I believe that anyone *can* find meaning in their work life without having to join a worthy nonprofit organization like the Peace Corps or drop out of the world of work altogether.

I had support from a variety of individuals whose wisdom and insights helped me create a deeply meaningful and fulfilling work life. I feel grateful to be able to pass along their wisdom in the hopes that those who follow can look in the mirror at the end of their careers, smile broadly, and say to themselves, "My work life mattered."

If you want your work life to matter more than the money you earn, then you need to know where to look. Only you can define what matters. Only you can know, in your heart of hearts, whether you are satisfied, or even proud, of the work you do, the way you do it, and who you do it with.

No one can give you a work life worthy of half of your waking hours. Only you can do that. But those who have gone before me left a breadcrumb trail. In this book, I have tried to honor their gifts to me by sharing those breadcrumbs with you.

Of course, work and life are messy, and they cannot be separated. What happens at home shapes your work, and what happens at work shapes who you are at home. At the center of your work life is you. And that means that shaping your work life is a huge part of shaping your whole life.

This book is not about success or, ultimately, about me. It is about what *you* want your life's work to mean when your days are done. It is about having integrity with yourself, having self-respect, and meeting the needs of those you love and care for, starting with yourself. In the end, it is about how your choices in your work life shape who you are as a human being.

I've written this book for the person I was when someone first suggested to me that there could be more to work than working. I was twenty-eight, had had some level of early career success, and was working for my third employer.

On the surface, everything seemed to be going well, but I had a nagging sense that there had to be more to work than just crossing tasks off my to-do list. I didn't know what more I was looking for, but

I sensed that something was missing, and I had no idea what that was or how I was going to find it.

I hope this book will help you become aware of what you want from work, how it can aid your growth as a person and as a professional, and how you can hold your head high in virtually any situation, knowing that you have the tools to navigate even the most challenging moments with confidence.

Since this subject is so deeply personal and so crucially important to every person who cares to explore the inner world of work, I have chosen to share my personal stories with candor and authenticity. This is not a book about how wonderful I am and how wonderful you should be. I am not suggesting that you follow my example—quite the opposite. In fact, I am asking you to hang with me through the first section of the book where I describe the rough early years of my career. You'll see that I benefited from being the oldest son of the founder of Vertex. You'll probably think I didn't earn my success.

Eventually, later in the book, you'll see my shame and self-judgment around these issues and the personal and professional growth that came from grappling with them. But if I don't show you where I started from, warts and all, you might not understand the process of how to figure out what matters most to you even when things aren't going the way you hoped they would.

What I am sharing are the hard lessons of struggle so that as you face your own hard moments, you can have confidence that there is hope and that often the most difficult moments are the ones that teach us the most.

After each story, there is a short set of reflections on my experience with the benefit of hindsight from my forty-year work life. Following these reflections are simple suggestions of action items that you can apply, on your own or with the help of a friend, to help you navigate similar circumstances should they arise as you make your way toward the work life of your dreams.

And why not have the work life of your dreams? Who said you can't? And if not now, when? It is not about climbing the ladder. It is about knowing the rungs that answer the question burning within each of us: Why am I here?

THRIVING IN THE ERA OF ARTIFICIAL INTELLIGENCE

I believe artificial intelligence (AI) to be the most powerful tool yet devised by humanity. Artificial intelligence can do incredible things, and I encourage you to find credible guidance on how to best utilize AI for the endless purposes for which it is well suited.

What it cannot do is decide what you choose to care about. It can inform and influence and help you determine and express that choice, but in the end only you can feel a genuine desire to serve a purpose that you believe in. Artificial intelligence is just that, a nonliving, mechanized, hyperpowerful *intelligence*. It does not have a *heart* or a *soul*. It cannot love or care for others nor can it feel loved or cared for. It can write as though it cares or loves, but it is not capable of genuine feelings of love, care, or commitment. It is not an "I," "he," "she," or "they"; it is a computer system.

Imagine floating in a pristine mountain lake, feeling the gentle waves slide by as you watch a glorious sunset slowly melting into the treetops on the far shore, the last rays of a perfect summer day sneaking through the branches, sparkling on the surface of the lake, temporarily blinding you as the breeze stills, creating a perfect silence as an inner serenity fills your soul.

Artificial intelligence could write that paragraph as though it were in that lake, but it could never feel water and wind, and it cannot ever experience the serenity it is writing about, however convincingly. Only a human can.

Artificial intelligence can inform, challenge, coach, celebrate, and help you. It can also mislead or confuse you if aren't careful about the underlying assumptions it may make in formulating its conclusions.

Please remember, artificial intelligence is like fire. If it is well managed, it can transform life for the better. If it is set free to do whatever it wants, unquestioned and unrestrained, it may well scorch everything in its path, including your work life.

I believe that we are living in a remarkable moment in history, where technology is in the process of changing everything, like it has before. In times like these, our sense of self, our confidence in who we are and what we believe in, is paramount. This deeply felt, inner knowing and the confidence that comes with it gives us the ability to successfully navigate uncertain waters.

Get ready to set sail on your voyage to the work life of your dreams, knowing one moment the lake is still and all is peaceful. The next, a hurricane rises over the opposite crest. Anchoring yourself in the confidence of not only knowing but feeling what is most important to you will help guide you to brighter shores ahead.

ABOUT THE ACTION STEPS

The action steps at the end of each chapter are my effort to distill the essence of what I have learned from my experience into commonsense actions that anyone can take to gain more fulfillment from a similar situation.

These steps aren't a program. There is no particular sequence to follow. Each chapter and set of action steps stands alone. No outcome is being sought other than the general attainment of greater personal meaning and fulfillment from your work than you might have had otherwise.

I have consulted with mental health professionals to check whether these simple steps represent any potential for harm. They have assured me that, properly understood as nonprofessional suggestions born of my experience, they do not have any more risk than hearing advice from a friend or colleague.

Please use these action steps as you see fit. Some of these suggestions will have no application to your unique work life experience now or in the future. Others may provide exactly the small bit of support you may need to navigate situations similar to those I share in this book.

In some cases, it will become evident that something more than these action steps is required. I encourage you to reach out to an experienced friend, colleague, family member, doctor, spiritual leader, or counselor to talk through any major work life decisions.

Do not rely solely on the action steps, or AI, when facing a potentially life-changing challenge or choice. And if you experience challenges with drugs or alcohol, have difficulty meeting commitments to loved ones, or find yourself considering harm to yourself or others, please seek professional help immediately. Qualified resources are noted in the appendix.

Thanks for listening and enjoy the journey!

JEFF WESTPHAL

WHO THE WHY AM I?

W_hy_ is a loaded word. School teaches us to answer the question "Why?" with the facts we are supposed to know or the rationale we are supposed to have on the tip of our tongue.

Why did the United States enter World War II? Because the Japanese attacked Pearl Harbor and the US sought to help defend the democratic world. Why did you choose to go to the state college? Because they offered a well-known program in my chosen field and it was more affordable than private college, plus I am a big fan of the basketball team.

But _why_ means so much more than the historic facts or the rationale for a decision. Asking the question Why? is a gateway to an endless journey of self-discovery. As we seek to understand the _whys_ of our lives, including our careers, we often find many layers and nuances that contribute to our choices, some of which we are well aware of and others, not so much!

Meaning is more than the dictionary definition. Meaning is a combination of facts, knowledge, analysis, feelings, beliefs, experience, and if you stick with it long enough, perhaps even wisdom.

At the dawn of my working life, I had no idea of the meaning, the why, of my work. Meaning was simply assumed, and had I been asked why I was going to work at an advertising agency in account management, my answer would have been, "Our neighbor said he thought I would be good at it, it seems like fun, and it was the best job I could get." I had no more sense of the meaning of my work than that.

After having been given the gift of the question: What is your purpose at work? and the opportunity to seriously explore this all-important question, the door to a world of wonder opened, and it hasn't closed since. Welcome to that open door.

What does your work mean to you?

I encourage you to explore this simple and eternal question with an attitude of wonder. There is no right answer, and you won't get any grade from anyone but yourself.

This is my way of paying forward the gift so freely given to me, four decades ago. May it give you the tremendous sense of satisfaction and fulfillment that it's given me every step of the way.

CHAPTER 1

GET A JOB!

In the early 1980s, I was a typical self-absorbed recent graduate from a suburban high school. Then I went off to college at the University of Richmond and discovered that the world is not as it seems.

In my jeans, sneakers, and crusty T-shirt, I sat spellbound as the class discussed recent news about government-backed Central American death squads murdering civilians. I was absolutely stunned and shocked at what I was hearing. US-trained vigilante death squads were killing scores of Guatemalans. How could that be?

Like many college sophomores, I was naive when it came to global geopolitics or anything other than sports. While growing up in the leafy suburbs of Philadelphia's Main Line, I didn't run across many classes on subjects like Central American death squads.

My sociology professor, Dr. Ted Lewellen, vividly described how the US government supported a military-backed dictatorship and actively trained death squads that caused an outrageous amount of human suffering. Eventually, more than two hundred thousand Guatemalans were killed over a thirty-six-year period.

I could not believe that my country was not only backing dictators in South America but actively helping them to violently repress their people. Something clicked inside me. I knew that this was not right and that I needed to do something about it.

Many deep conversations with professors, family, and like-minded friends opened a whole new world to me. I spent many evenings at the home of Dr. Lewellen's close friend, Dr. Martin Ryle, a professor of Russian history, where a group of us gathered as Dr. Ryle asked us thought-provoking questions and let us debate them until the wee hours.

I channeled my considerable passion and energy into the global human rights organization Amnesty International, volunteering and eventually leading the University of Richmond chapter. We organized events, sent out mailings, distributed literature, and recruited volunteers in support of a number of global initiatives.

It was the first time I had been connected to a cause, and with my extroverted personality and considerable energy and verbal acuity, I was able to have an impact. Most importantly, being a leader for a worthy cause gave me the satisfaction that I was doing something meaningful that could benefit not only me but those who were in true need.

Volunteering with Amnesty International opened my eyes. I saw that the world was mysterious and flawed and in drastic need of positive change. With my youthful altruism now energized and focused, I would come home from college and pepper my parents with stories about how the United States did not care enough about the people being abused by their own governments.

"Did you hear about this?" I would lecture them. "We are actually helping these guys torture their own people!"

Worn down by their newly idealistic son, they no doubt hoped that "this too shall pass."

And pass it did.

After I graduated from the University of Richmond, my focus completely shifted away from my volunteer work with Amnesty International. With it went my strong desire to make a difference in the world. Not long afterward, my transition from passionate, idealistic college student to an ambitious young career professional effectively buried my altruistic urge beneath a blanket of blind ambition.

After partying my way into dropping out of law school and having the quintessential—and well deserved—"get a job" talk from my father, I began looking for professional work in Washington, DC, where I was living after graduation. A neighbor suggested that I consider advertising and helped to arrange some interviews. With persistence, I landed a job as a junior account executive at a major advertising agency in Washington, DC.

I now focused all my energy on climbing the career ladder. My first rung was to sell Hechinger paint and hardware to upscale Washingtonians. Then, after a move back to Philadelphia to join another leading ad agency, I shifted my focus to marketing Embassy Suites hotel rooms and hotel amenities to business travelers on behalf of the Scott Paper Company, which was later acquired by Kimberly-Clark.

I was on top of the world serving big-name clients. Hechinger, Embassy Suites, and Scott Paper were all household names in the 1980s and 1990s. I had a career, and it was exciting. I had entered the rat race, never once thinking for an instant about whether the work I was doing made a difference to anyone, least of all myself. My sole concern was to meet my clients' expectations. The battle was intense, and I was blinded by the fight.

At the time, my job felt like it offered me a simple, easy equation. My corporate clients needed to sell products and services. I needed to help them. I was not sure why, but the need burned hot. It was challenging and fun and, as it turned out, I was pretty good at it.

It never dawned on me that I, like so many before me, had completely abandoned my desire to make a difference in the world in exchange for simply finding a place in that world.

Late one afternoon, I was standing by the outdoor grill with my father, cooking steaks, when I announced that I had accepted a position with the Marriott Corporation to lead their marketing efforts for the Roy Rogers restaurant chain in the Baltimore/DC area. This was a major career opportunity and meant settling in the DC area and moving in with Jenifer, then my fiancée.

My father listened quietly and then said, "Why don't you come to work at Vertex?" I was shocked. Those were the first words he'd ever said to me about joining his own business providing sales tax compliance data and software to US businesses.

As dazed and confused as I was, I immediately said, "OK," like a drowning man might immediately grab a life preserver. I didn't even consider talking to Jenifer about it before saying yes. Just like that, at age twenty-six, I became the director of marketing for Vertex, Inc., employee #29. Without a moment of thought or consulting a single soul, I agreed to join the family business.

REFLECTION

At least twenty years passed before I realized that my knee-jerk decision to accept my father's offer was all about wanting acceptance from him. I am still amazed that I made such a decision with absolutely no career plan, no vision of my future, and no concept of what it might mean to join my father's company.

What's worse is that it wasn't just a career decision. It was a personal decision that set my career and my life on a path I could not have imagined. Yet it didn't occur to me to discuss this with my fiancée, mother, sisters, a close friend, or anybody for that matter. I finally came to understand that not only did that decision totally change my career and my life, but it substantially impacted the lives of everyone around me.

It did not start well. The first few years were almost unbearable. My father and I did not see eye to eye on just about anything. I thought of resigning on numerous occasions even as the company grew rapidly, in some part due to my contributions.

In the advertising business, where my energy and creativity were a perfect match, I was a fish swimming in comfortable waters. In the tax software field, I was more like a fish climbing a mountain, surrounded by the billy goats who had forgotten more about taxation and technology than I had ever known.

The fact that it turned out well does not mean that I couldn't have managed the situation more effectively. With the benefit of hindsight, I know that a few simple steps could have led to a much more meaningful and fulfilling experience for everyone involved, most significantly, my wife and family.

ACTION STEPS—TAKING TIME TO MAKE MORE MEANINGFUL DECISIONS

While you may never face the same scenario—a parent asking an adult child to join a family business—you may well face any number of similar situations where a significant opportunity or dilemma presents itself seemingly out of nowhere, and you feel you should respond immediately.

The reality is that very few decisions need to be made instantaneously. Life-changing career decisions especially require time to explore what it would mean for your future and for the futures of those you care about. When faced with a similarly significant career decision, try following these six steps and see if they help you arrive at a more meaningful and satisfying outcome.

1. What is being proposed?

2. Why are you interested in the proposal? What opportunity would it open up for you both personally and professionally?

3. What future outcomes are you hoping will be realized if you were to move forward?

4. Discuss the situation with an experienced individual who is not involved.

5. Discuss what you learn with those who are involved, like a significant other.

6. You are now ready to make an informed, well-thought-out decision!

AI NOTE: You may want to use AI to gather the knowledge you may need to better evaluate the situation. AI can help you imagine scenarios that might unfold were you to pursue different alternatives.

CHAPTER 2

IMPOSTER? WHO, ME?

Instead of showing up at the Marriott Corporation in Maryland to join their marketing team, I was showing up at the company my father had founded and nursed into being. I was filling a new position, director of marketing, created just for the boss's son. The nepotism was obvious to everyone, including me.

I was torn. Having always done as well as I cared to do in school and having had a fair amount of success in the competitive advertising world, I was not lacking confidence in my ability to achieve. And, with a few prior summers working in sales at my father's company under my belt, I felt like I had a general understanding of the business.

At the same time, I was uncomfortable with the obvious fact that I had not gotten this job because of my past accomplishments. This job was given to me because I was the founder's son.

Certainly, my father would not have offered me a job if I had no meaningful prior success or ability. At the same time, there was no competitive interview process, there were no other candidates, and he did not ask any of the other employees for their opinion about whether the role was needed or if I was a fit for it. This was a classic case of a founder father wanting his son to join the business and succeed him, just as had been done for countless generations in the old Europe of his heritage.

I had known all the current employees by first name for many years before my first official day on the job in the fall of 1988. From the outset, I felt like I should apologize to everyone for even being there. Part of me was excited about the opportunity to prove myself to my father, and the other part was embarrassed that I had this instantaneous influence for which I was not fully qualified or prepared.

The only way I had of coping with this contradiction was a combination of working like a madman, partying like a madman, and being as nice as I could be, often apologizing for imagined transgressions.

Against this confused emotional backdrop, we grew like crazy. The combination of audit demands on corporations and a major innovation in our product offering led to an explosion in revenue, quadrupling the business in just four years. I arrived at the company in 1988 as employee #29 in a business doing about $4.5 million in annual revenue. By 1992, the company had nearly seventy-five employees and revenues of $16 million. Our success, driven largely by forces beyond our control, gave us all, and me in particular, a sense that we would succeed at anything we set our sights on.

The company's success also led to a nice bonus, and Jenifer and I were able to purchase our dream home, a lovely ninety-year-old Dutch colonial with a nice lot only two miles from the office. Our daughter, Annie, was born two weeks after we moved in—just enough time for the one-time professional painter (*me*) to patch, caulk, and paint the interior.

After losing two babies to ectopic pregnancy in the years after Annie's birth, we were graced with Kyle in 1992 after two months of early labor. Jake would arrive two years later, after yet another bout of early labor.

My father, Ray Westphal, had grown up above the family's interior design store in the working-class neighborhood of Pelham, New York.

From those roots, he became the founder, CEO, and owner of the fast-growing tax technology business, Vertex. Ray Westphal had made it, and he had done it his way.

My father had achieved this success even though he was never a people person. Now, through the success of his business, he had realized the American dream and was ready to reap the rewards. Seeing that I was doing well in my role, he headed to the golf course and world destinations with my mother, basking in the glow of his hard work and well-earned good fortune.

What he did not see, and what I did not understand, was the stress that all this success was creating within me. Although I was excited by it and felt as though I was contributing my fair share of the effort, I still felt deeply conflicted. I was two decades younger and less experienced than my peers, and I had also become the informal but evident successor. It wasn't fair. I knew it. They knew it. But none of us could talk about it.

It was like driving blindfolded at one hundred miles per hour with the brakes pressed to the floor and smoke billowing out from under the hood, and the only thing that could cool the engine was a constant stream of alcohol and a pinch of tobacco between my cheek and gum.

REFLECTION

In my late twenties and early thirties I had no idea what stress was, where it came from, or what I might be able to do about it. The notion that I might have been experiencing anxiety, which is well understood among young adults today, would not have made sense to me at the time.

What I thought I was doing was winning at the game of life, and I thought that winning meant going hard. What I thought I was experiencing wasn't stress or anxiety, it was the challenge of winning at home, in business, and at the party.

I did not realize that my goals were in serious opposition to each other. I wanted to be a good husband and father, which meant being more sensitive and understanding than my adult male role models had been when I was growing up.

I also wanted to succeed in my work, prove to my father that I was more capable than he thought I was, and at the same time never become a serious businessman, which I saw as someone who became dead to the joy of living. I pledged to myself that I would not succumb to a numbing, obedient, and meaningless working life. That pledge meant that I would continue to be the life of the party, and I would do everything I could to bring that life-of-the-party energy into my work life as well.

I was vaguely aware of these inner aspirations as I careened from one overcommitment to the next. What I was not aware of was how much damage those implicit commitments were doing to my relationships, both at home and at work, as well as to my health. Even my persistent lower back pain didn't trigger any sense in me that something was out of kilter. It was merely the price one had to pay to go big or go home. When I looked at my life at age thirty, I saw that I had a beautiful and driven life partner, a precocious and brilliant eldest daughter, a delightful first son, a classic little starter home complete with the white picket fence, and sales going through the roof. It seemed like I had cornered the market on the good life. And yet, while I drank beer and chewed tobacco while working after the family had gone to bed, I had this nagging sense that something was not quite right. They have a term for this pattern today. It's called burnout, and I was a classic case of someone headed for a major meltdown.

ACTION STEPS—TAKING STOCK

I did not know how to pause and take stock of my work life when I could have benefited from it most. Just a few quiet minutes to myself with some simple questions and a bit of input from my colleagues and loved ones might have offered me valuable perspective, and perhaps I could have avoided some of the more painful lessons that were yet to come.

If I had known how to pause and take stock, these are questions I could have asked myself. I offer you the opportunity to ask yourself the following questions:

1. What is working well in your work life?

2. Are you experiencing any discomfort or unwanted strain? If so, what is it, and why do you think it is happening?

3. Can you ask a trusted colleague, family member, or close friend to share their perspective on these two questions?

4. With the awareness you have developed by thinking about questions 1–3, continue to reflect each week on what might be fueling what is working and what is creating discomfort, and most importantly, why.

AI NOTE: You may want to utilize a software tool, which may rely on AI, to help you track and analyze your reflections over time. Beware that anything you say or write online is discoverable forever. Choose your online resources carefully, ensuring full compliance with data security standards and regulations.

CHAPTER 3

OUT OF THE BLUE

Back then nearly everyone in the Philadelphia metropolitan area read *The Philadelphia Inquirer*. When a reporter who covered small businesses for the paper asked to interview my father, we were all flattered by the attention and excited for the opportunity.

It was the perfect feel-good story for a columnist who specialized in regional small business stories. And I was a bit surprised and proud that my father asked me to join him in the interview. We didn't even think of engaging any public relations help in preparation.

When the big day arrived, the interviewer began by asking some predictable background-oriented questions. I knew better than to chime in with my own comments and just listened politely as the interviewer asked my father about how the business got started and what the products did—getting grounded in our business.

What happened next came as a complete surprise.

"What are your plans for the future of the company, Ray?" asked the journalist. My dad paused and said, "Jeff will succeed me as CEO of the company."

It was a good thing that I had not taken a big swig of my Coke just then, or it would have been sprayed all over the room. My eyes must have looked like basketballs. Just as when he cornered me at the grill and dropped the "Why not come work at Vertex?" on me, he was dropping the successor news on me without ever having said a word about it.

Not. One. Single. Word.

My thoughts cycled through *Yes!* then *Oh no!* then *Yes!* and again, *Oh no!* I am not gonna lie—it felt good to receive my father's approval, even though I also felt enormous anxiety.

I immediately thought about my colleagues who were all about twenty years my senior. They had built the company with him and were about to learn this news in the next morning's newspaper!

I kept my mouth shut as the reporter finished the interview. Dad thanked him and motioned for me to see the gentleman out of the office, which I did. The reporter thanked me and congratulated me in reference to the news about my evident succession. I thanked him for his time and said goodbye.

As soon as he turned away, I spun around and bolted back to my father's office, quickly and quietly shutting the door. He looked up, surprised to see me there, as if he'd expected me to just go back to work as though nothing had happened.

"Dad," I said, "I don't know what to say. Thank you for the confidence you have in me. But I think you'd better consider how Frank, Jon, Tome', Jack, and Bill are going to feel when they read this news in the paper tomorrow."

Now it was his turn to have eyeballs the size of basketballs! He blinked, blinked again, gulped, regained his composure, and said, "Thank you. Good point. I was planning to talk to them about it."

I realized it had never dawned on him to talk to anyone about it, not even my mother or my sisters. It felt good to be of some help in that moment. I got up and left. The article was extremely favorable. And right there in black and white was the news that I would succeed my father and lead the company someday.

REFLECTION

We all have moments when surprising news arrives. A colleague leaves the company. A parent becomes ill and needs care that impacts the family's finances and career commitments. A life partner has a career opportunity that impacts your own career options.

What I experienced on that day was a mixture of shock, excitement, concern, fear, and confusion. Despite this mishmash of feelings, I believed that it wouldn't change me. Only now, after years of work to learn how to understand and accept my feelings, can I identify how I felt on that day.

What the news meant to me was that my work was being appreciated by my father, something that I had never felt before. At the same time, I knew that I was expected to succeed him primarily because I was his son, not because I was qualified, since I clearly wasn't.

Eventually, I also realized that the news meant wildly different things to everyone involved.

Did I realize the impact on my family of origin, all of whom had worked or were working in the company at the time?

Nope. Not a clue. I was completely blind to the implications for my mother and sisters, something that I regret to this day.

Did I realize what I would be signing Jenifer and my kids up for?

Nope. Not a clue. Only later would my wife and I acknowledge that I had married the company, not just her.

I slowly came to understand that leading an organization isn't just a job. The sense of responsibility one feels for the well-being of all involved makes the role completely inseparable from the entirety of one's life. There isn't a moment when a thought about the business couldn't emerge and immediately consume my attention—because there is never enough time for all the people who want your time and attention at work. How I spent my time was a constant test of my priorities between care for my family, my colleagues, and myself.

Of course, as I think back on this now, I know that it's likely true for many work roles that people fulfill. Whether you are contacted to fill a shift as a barista at the local coffee shop or to stay on call in the ER as an anesthesiologist, all sorts of jobs require a constant balancing act between self, home, and work. Try as we might, I don't think we can take the self out of work or the work out of self, regardless of where we are, what time it is, or what we are doing at the moment.

What I did realize was that my peers in the company, the people who had supported my father's dream and made that dream a reality through a deep commitment to their work, were about to find out that a young man of thirty-two, with three years of advertising agency experience and five years of tax technology industry experience, was at some point going to be their boss.

What is fascinating to me now was that, at the time, we had absolutely no conversation that I was a part of about my father's announcement within the company or the family. Jen and I talked about it, and we were certainly encouraged. But it never dawned on me that my father or I should initiate a conversation about his statement about me succeeding him with the family or our colleagues at work.

I can only imagine what the reactions, feelings, and assumptions of others might have been at the time. I wish that I had had the wisdom then to have sought out their perspectives. So much could have been learned that would have made the eventual transition much more manageable, effective, and respectful of everyone involved.

ACTION STEPS—IMPACT ASSESSMENT

Events mean different things to different people at different times. As you prepare for future news about your career, whatever that news might be, consider the following questions and steps to help you process the information in a way that supports the fulfillment you seek in your work life.

Here are some questions that may help you.

1. What happened?

2. Why did it happen? What do you actually know as a fact, and what are your speculations about why it happened?

3. What does it mean to you that this event has happened? How do you feel about what has happened?

4. What might this news mean to others who are impacted? Might others see the news differently than you do? If so, why might that be? Is there a domino effect where the news that impacts you directly may impact others indirectly through you?

5. Share your observations with those close to you and seek their perspectives before taking action.

AI NOTE: AI is not recommended to support this self-reflective activity.

CHAPTER 4

UGLY WRAPPING PAPER

By 1992 Vertex was a small but rapidly growing business serving major US corporations as they endured significant audit pressure from state governments that could result in penalties and interest totaling millions of dollars. Vertex was the original and leading innovator of technology solutions to meet this demand, and we had grown fourfold in four years.

Business was good, and I was having a blast. Our fledgling company was as fast and furious a work environment as one could have imagined. We had no strategy. We had no performance goals other than to sell more. We had no organization chart, no budget, and no compensation philosophy other than when times were good, my father would announce a special bonus or take everyone on a trip.

We did have chutzpah, a can-do attitude, and a willingness to take almost any risk in the name of meeting a customer's need and growing the business. It was energizing, exciting, and rewarding. But if I had known then what I know now, I would have shouted, "SLOW DOWN!"

But we did not slow down. Instead, we kept pushing forward in fast and furious mode.

Then it happened. In the fall of 1992, we suffered a major setback when a promising new software product failed in its initial release and had to be withdrawn from the market.

There was a significant breakdown in understanding the readiness of the software to take on the demands of major corporations. The left hand did not adequately understand what the right hand was doing. This led us to a major customer disappointment.

It was a black eye for the company and a profound shock to my system. After much reflection, I came to realize that we had failed primarily due to a lack of ability to work together effectively, or as it is commonly known today, to collaborate.

We were devastated. The admission of defeat and the recall of the product was embarrassing for the company and humiliating for me personally. It was the end of a period when it seemed anything we touched would turn to gold.

Yet, as painful as it was, the new product recall was exactly what we needed. We were out of control, overcommitted, and exhausted. The way of working that my father had successfully put into motion was quickly becoming obsolete. It was a clear case of how a strength could also be a great weakness, as our zeal for growth at all costs had led us to run the business without the much-needed controls and discipline in place to avoid such a disaster.

REFLECTION

The greatest gifts sometimes come in ugly wrapping paper. What worked for us in the past was not guaranteed to be what we needed to move forward. Facing our flaws and embracing change after a humiliating defeat was not easy, but it was necessary.

Until we were forced to pick up the pieces from the new product recall, we had no sense of our future aspirations, no strategy to speak of, no financial forecasts, and not a single shred of awareness about the culture we wanted to create. It turned out that our big adversity was a great big gift because it sent us back to the drawing board, challenging us to build a company that would not embarrass itself.

In the months and years afterward, I learned to question everything I thought I knew about business, especially my own limitations. It marked the beginning of a continuous search for a better me and a better way to be at work. Until then, my career had been a series of successes, and I certainly had the ego to match.

It was like riding a long, flowing ocean wave only to be dashed on a set of rocks you did not see on the shore. We were lucky and withstood the product failure. Now it was time to learn from our mistakes.

ACTION STEPS—LEARNING FROM ADVERSITY

Nobody has a perfect radar. The world of work is too complex for that, and it would be exhausting and defeating to try to control a future that is in a constant state of flux. What you can do is learn from experience to prepare for future unplanned developments.

Toward that end, consider these simple steps to enhance your agility and growth to prepare for the next time you are confronted with an adverse experience that surprises and disappoints you.

1. Reflect on your past work life and identify an adverse experience that surprised and disappointed you.

2. Why were you surprised? Why were you disappointed?

3. What did you learn from that experience?

4. How did you apply that learning?

5. Drawing from this reflection, what are three things you want to be prepared to feel, think, or do if you are disappointed by another unexpected development?

AI NOTE: This activity is best experienced without the help of AI.

CHAPTER 5

SURVEY SAYS!

Before the new product debacle, I didn't think I needed any help and assumed we were simply going to keep on growing, thanks mostly to some magic touch I believed we had. But failure has a strange way of leading you to the proverbial crossroads.

While we were able to redirect quite a few of the people we had recently hired to work on the new software product into roles within the established business, we could not see a way to keep everyone. In the end, some innocent and caring people were let go, adding a deep emotional scar on top of the humiliation we all felt at having failed with the new product.

We were demoralized. But, at the same time, the 1991 recession moved into the rearview mirror, and demand for our flagship sales tax solution was as strong as ever. Within months I was so consumed by our growth opportunities, it was as though the new product failure was ancient history.

That is except for this nagging feeling that something was fundamentally wrong. We had been succeeding, but perhaps despite ourselves. I knew I needed help. For me to admit that was a game changer, both personally and professionally.

One of our earliest employees, Paul Beirnes, suggested I might talk to his father-in-law, who was a former IBMer turned management consultant. His name was Bill North. Bill was your classic IBM salesperson—tall, athletic, and handsome, with a ready smile and easy laugh and always sporting the ubiquitous white button-down shirt and tie.

Bill turned me on to one of the most popular business, leadership, and personal development books of all time, *The 7 Habits of Highly Effective People* by Stephen Covey. After immersing myself in Covey, I read the seminal work on collaboration, *The Wisdom of Teams* by Jon Katzenbach and Doug Smith.

Those books convinced me that the answer to what had doomed our new software product was a lack of communication and teamwork throughout the company. In particular, Covey's principle of "seeking first to understand" seemed to be the missing link.

Building teamwork would be a sharp departure from the typical entrepreneur-as-monarch approach we had employed until then. As the would-be CEO, it was important that I walk the talk. Bill was willing to help.

Bill's first step was to give me the Covey 360° diagnostic evaluation (now the FranklinCovey 360° Assessment). This evaluation consists of sending a survey to my stakeholders in the business: my coworkers, other leaders, my father, and the sales and marketing team of six employees I was leading at the time. The diagnostic asks questions about quality of work and treatment of coworkers and includes character-based questions about listening, trust, and other leadership attributes and skills.

With the compiled input in hand in the form of a report, Bill had a look of anticipation on his face when he handed it to me. At the time, I was certain that everyone understood and was grateful for all the hard work and long hours I put in on their behalf. I was looking forward to seeing just how much I was appreciated.

We were reviewing the findings and came to the ultimate leadership question in the survey—"Do you trust this person?" My overall rating was a 3 out of 7 on a scale where 1 was "not at all" and 7 was "completely."

I was devastated.

Clearly in denial, I could not believe it at first. I thought, *The people I am killing myself for gave me a 3 out of 7 on trust! How could that be? That has got to be wrong.*

Bill explained it to me: "Jeff, there is what you know, there is what you know you don't know, and then there is what you don't know you don't know." What I did not know I did not know was that people did not trust me. I needed to understand why, and I needed to know ASAP!

Bill and I dug into the rest of the feedback, and it turned out my lack of listening skills was a big part of the problem. Also, I learned that in my overzealous quest to get things done, I often trampled on other employees' feelings and opinions or did not even bother to seek them out in the first place. I believed it was their job to ask me for decisions and my job to make them.

Involving my employees in the decision-making process itself had never even occurred to me.

Because I was completely focused on my "doing," I had no awareness of my state of being and how this was impacting those around me. When I realized it was more meaningful for our employees to be treated as partners in the process, my whole approach to leadership shifted.

The work became less important, and our workers became much more important. I slowly began to see entirely new dimensions in the meaning of the work I was doing, the inner motivation that was driving me, and the impact I was having on others.

I began to put into practice Covey's seven habits with empathic listening right at the top. It was a game changer for me, the executive team, and eventually the entire organization. And it happened just in time.

REFLECTION

The change in me was fundamental. While I had always felt uncertain of myself, never feeling as confident as I tried to appear, a score of 3 out of 7 was undeniable evidence that something essential was not right. I didn't know what it was, but I couldn't deny that something major about my work life wasn't working.

The FranklinCovey 360° Assessment gave me the shock I needed to start reflecting on my own behavior. While difficult, it was one of the most meaningful experiences of my early career, and I am deeply grateful to my colleagues for their honesty.

My self-image at the time was that I was deeply committed, hard-working, and devoted to serving the company and my colleagues. I believed I was honest and, most importantly, that I deeply cared for everyone as fellow human beings. As the son of the founder and owner, I felt guilty, even ashamed, about my unique privilege, which fueled an obsessive need to try and do everything I could for everyone involved.

That is who I thought I was and who I thought others believed me to be. As it turned out, the way I was behaving was creating a vastly different impression on others than the impression I wanted them to have. Once the results came back and I realized that who I was trying to be was not who I was perceived to be, I had to find out why and make the necessary changes.

From where I sit today, decades later, it is obvious to me now that I was straddling two competing visions of who I should be: my father's vision of the commandeering, larger-than-life leader, and my mother's vision of a more sensitive, caring, and humane form of leadership, where serving others was the best way to succeed.

Covey's seven habits showed me a hybrid vision that integrated the two seemingly contradictory ideals. Using my unique privilege and singular authority to create an environment where people could work better together offered a means to reconcile these two competing worldviews while relieving some of the pressure I was feeling to live up to two apparently contradictory mandates.

ACTION STEPS—SEEING YOURSELF MORE CLEARLY

Many high-quality resources are available to individuals who want to better understand how they are perceived by those around them (see the resources in the appendix). And, if you want to take action on your own, here are some simple steps you can follow.

1. Write down who you think you are at work. Start your own paragraph with "My self-image is . . ."

2. Ask a trusted friend or colleague to interview four coworkers, including one person senior to you, simply asking them, "How do you experience my friend/colleague at work?"

3. Meet with your friend and remind yourself that feedback is being provided out of a desire to help you. Then take a deep breath and really listen to your friend as they share the results of the interviews.

4. Talk with your friend and choose one thing that emerged from the interviews that you can do differently to improve your relationships at work. Give it some time, six to twelve weeks, and check back in with those who provided input to help assess your progress.

AI NOTE: I recommend working with a real person, rather than an AI bot, for this experience. The feedback you are looking for is about how you show up with others as a human being at work as well as how work influences your life when not actively working. This is about the quality of your relationships.

A trusted friend, family member, or colleague can have a much higher-quality conversation with the people in your orbit than what AI could tell you from reading your social media, emails, or survey results. Feedback surveys like the one Bill facilitated for me can be helpful, but without a Bill to help you process the feedback, you may not gain the insight that can benefit you most, and you may come to conclusions that are unwise.

CHAPTER 6

WHEN THE STUDENT IS READY

Deflated yet emboldened by the feedback, I asked Bill to provide me with more active coaching, but he declined. His other clients were demanding too much of his time. Instead, he introduced me to a former DuPont executive named Jim Patton.

Six years earlier, Jim had suffered a major heart attack. After recovering, he'd stepped off the C-level fast track and redirected his career to what was a radical idea in the 1980s. He would become a resource to help other DuPont executives become more effective leaders and hold more effective meetings.

In this line of work, Jim had become a certified Stephen Covey 7 Habits facilitator and was proficient in other leadership strategies and philosophies as well. He facilitated meetings, including those conducted by DuPont's CEO at the time. Then, after DuPont suffered a business downturn and let go of all their executive resource people, including Jim, he became an independent consultant.

Based on Bill's confident referral, I hired Jim to help our fledgling leadership group become a more cohesive and effective team. He joined our weekly meetings and facilitated our discussions on how to work together more effectively. Before and after the meetings, Jim coached me on how to play my role as team leader, as by this time I had become executive vice president of the company.

Over the six months of getting to know each other, I marveled at who this man was. Nothing I said seemed to faze him at all. He spoke no opinion of his own about anything. I felt like there was nothing I could say or do that he would judge or criticize.

I had never met anyone like him in my life. In addition to being remarkably calm, he was the most plain vanilla human being I'd ever encountered. He always wore well-polished penny loafers, brown khakis, a simple button-down shirt, and a preppy crew-neck sweater. And he drove a tan, late-model Honda civic sedan.

He was the polar opposite of an Elon Musk. There was something about him I couldn't describe or explain. He was a chemist, pastor, and therapist all rolled up into one person. I soon found myself feeling desperate to know what this man knew.

REFLECTION

I realize now that I wouldn't have been open to Jim's wisdom had I not experienced the dramatic failure of the product launch and the big aha from the FranklinCovey 360° Assessment feedback. Those experiences triggered a deep desire in me to change for the better, but I had no idea what I was trying to become or how to make the changes necessary. I knew I needed help, but I didn't know what help I needed.

That is when this unassuming character with more experience than I had ever imagined having walked into my life. In the context of the changes I was experiencing during that time, Jim proved to be a great fit. All he did was smile, make me feel comfortable, and listen as though every word I had to say was the most important thing he had ever heard. While Jim clearly practiced the art of "seek first to understand," I experienced him as more than that—much more. I felt something akin to pure acceptance from him, and I could not get enough of it.

What Jim did first was to model a state of being in constant appreciation, curiosity, and wonder at what he might learn next from me. Not once in our twenty years together did I feel him dismissing anything I had to say as though he already knew the right answer, and never once did I feel pushed toward what he thought was the right thing to do.

The second thing he did was challenge me, in the most patient and loving way, to clarify my purpose and vision at every level and to help me bring my unconscious motivations to the surface. Whether I was pondering an upcoming meeting, a new strategy, or the very existence of the business itself, his question was always some version of, "What purpose are you seeking to serve?"

ACTION STEPS—FINDING A MENTOR

It takes people with a special kind of patience and trust to be effective mentors. Many people are capable and would be honored to be your mentor, regardless of compensation. Here are some simple steps to find a mentor.

1. Do some research and create a profile of the kind of attributes you are looking for in a mentor. For example, is this person a good listener? Do they have work or life experience you respect? Do they possess wisdom that intrigues you?

2. Think about the people you know. Who might be a mentor candidate? Who might be in a position to know mentor candidates? Reach out to them and let them know you are seeking a mentor. See what happens.

    a. Remember, the mentor cannot be someone you work with or live with or socialize with. Perhaps a cousin, aunt, or former employer could serve in the role if you are not too closely connected. The mentor does not need to know anything about your business or your skills. In fact, it is better if they do not. Mentoring is not about subject matter expertise or advice. Mentoring is about process.

3. Talk with this person about what mentoring is or is not. Listen for opinions or advice that you have not specifically sought. Does the person ask you open-ended questions that make you curious?

4. Meet with your prospective mentor perhaps once a month. After three or four months, ask yourself, "Am I thinking in new ways about my work and aspirations?" and "Do I feel appreciated for who I am?" If your answer is yes, you have likely found a good mentor. If the answer isn't a clear yes, thank the person, move on, and keep looking for the right individual.

AI NOTE: AI coaches may prove to be highly effective. Some people report feeling appreciated or even loved by the expressions of an AI system. While the AI cannot actually love, it can be quite effective at demonstrating its understanding of your point of view. In a world where that skill is sorely lacking, being understood and appreciated, even by a machine, can feel refreshing. I recommend, however, a human being as a mentor for two reasons: First, a real person can truly care and you can genuinely feel their caring. Second, relating with a real person, as imperfect as all real people are, can help you grow in confidence in your other human relationships.

CHAPTER 7

RIDDLE ME THIS

Before and after the meetings and during coaching sessions, Jim often asked probing questions like "How do you plan to encourage spirit and willfulness?"

Spirit and willfulness? What the heck is that? I thought.

It was frustrating at first. Up to that point, the only time I'd ever been honestly asked, "Why?" was during evenings at the home of my college history professor, Dr. Martin Ryle, who played Socrates to a group of inquiring young minds, always asking questions about why and never answering them.

When I struggled with a certain problem or issue, Jim would repeatedly take me back to one of Covey's core principles: "Begin with the end in mind." Over and over, he would lead me to clarify my purpose and vision, often expanding on the question, "How do you intend to serve the greater whole?"

The greater what? The whole of what? I thought, profoundly confused, but curious. It soon became evident to me that Jim was using riddles to challenge me to think beyond my current assumptions. By asking me questions I didn't even understand, he knew that I had to step back and question my deeper assumptions, ones I didn't even know I had.

Jim repeatedly challenged me to think beyond my typical "problem–solution" dynamic and explore the more strategic bigger-picture implications of my decisions. With Jim's help, my leadership team and I began to discover and better understand the contextual dynamics surrounding the situations, processes, or decisions we were considering.

This was a huge shift from our unspoken assumption that "fixing problems faster" was our primary purpose. The customer had a problem, we had a solution, and the more customer problems we solved and the faster we solved them, the happier they would be and the more product they would buy. There was not much more "why" to it than that!

During the ten years of his facilitation and mentoring at Vertex, Jim would continue posing riddles. He was teaching me and my leadership team to see not only what was happening on the surface of events but to consider the impact and subtext of the relationships and motivations involved.

Slowly, we stopped battling each other and began to appreciate each other's differences and unique ways of looking at any situation. Our practice of reflecting on our process at the end of every meeting produced increasingly insightful, authentic, and appreciative sharing among team members and a way to see the world through the eyes of the others. And, by learning how to truly "see" each other, we began to see and understand ourselves better.

Slowly and steadily, Jim was encouraging me to discover what was meant by the old saying "There's more here than meets the eye."

Jim stretched my sense of vision beyond the road directly ahead, beyond even the visible horizon. He challenged me, in the most loving way, to ask myself, "What difference will my work have made when all is said and done?"

REFLECTION

Thanks to Jim's patient challenges, I discovered that what I thought I was doing was completely disconnected from the contribution I was making to the world around me. The meaning I experienced from the very same work went from "selling tax software" to "improving people's lives everywhere through tax software."

My altruistic urge, going back to my days in college volunteering for Amnesty International, was reunited with my work, and work no longer felt like work.

I became more open to the wisdom and facilitation of mentors, coaches, and guides. I realized I could not go on this journey alone without help. And I learned that help was all around me if I stayed open to possibilities when there appeared to be none and put into practice what I was learning in a continuous exploration of the possible.

Building on his challenge to get clear about my purpose and desired outcomes, Jim stretched my intentionality even further, asking me, "What future are you seeking to create?" This is a broader version of "What outcomes are you hoping to achieve?"

Thanks to Jim's mentoring, I learned that all my desired outcomes from our projects and strategies were just steps toward a much larger goal, a dream of the future I wanted to see realized, even if I was not fully conscious of what that future should be.

ACTION STEPS—WHAT FUTURE WORK LIFE AM I SEEKING TO CREATE?

You do not need to see a direct connection between your work and curing cancer to create a deeper sense of satisfaction, meaning, and fulfillment in what you do. It is enough to see a child learn something new that they can use in life, or to serve a table where a young couple is falling in love over dinner.

It need not be something life-changing, like it was for me. That said, when people do take a moment to connect the dots between what they do and the ultimate difference it makes, what they discover can be amazing.

You can use these steps to imagine the future work life you seek to create:

1. Briefly describe your current work life and what you find meaningful about it.

2. Describe the ideal work life you would like to realize in five to ten years.

3. If you feel adventurous, draw a picture of what that future work life looks like. The quality of the art does not matter.

4. Sit with a friend, family member, or colleague and share your thoughts with them, inviting them to ask questions to add depth to the vision you've just created.

5. Ask yourself, "Have I limited the scope of my vision because I've assumed particular limitations?" If so, let those limitations go, and repeat the process.

AI NOTE: AI can be extremely helpful for you in creating a vision of your ideal work life, particularly for those who feel less than confident in their artistic abilities. AI can help you research potential work and life possibilities. You might ask it: "How do people find meaning in careers like the one I am interested in?" or "What are the childcare options in the new city where I dream of living?" You can talk to an AI by describing your dream future and asking it to paint a mural representing the future you want. Just remember, the one thing AI cannot do for you is tell you what you should want or care about, and most importantly, why. That is your exclusive domain. Have fun!

CHAPTER 8

ACROSS THE CHOPPING BLOCK

Drawing upon Jim's example, it seemed clear to me that the only way to build a company founded on shared understanding and genuine, intrinsically meaningful commitment was to change my own behavior and strive to build shared understanding and true commitment in everything I did.

This was not going to be easy. At the time, my life was a 24/7/365 panic attack.

I would literally leap out of bed at five a.m. to get to the office before six a.m. so I would not be stuck in the house when our young children would arise. I left my wife, Jenifer, to fend for herself and the three kids.

I generally returned around seven p.m. in the evening. I would wolf down some dinner, play with the kids a bit, and help rush them off to bed so I could jump back on the computer and work until midnight before collapsing into bed, often waking in the middle of the night and working for an hour or more then too.

I lived about two miles from the office, so it was not as if I was spending two hours a day in traffic. I spent all that time away from my family at the office. In hindsight, it's no surprise that I suffered from chronic back pain through the entire period of my early marriage and early career. I often dragged my right leg around the office, half stooped over due to the ever-present stiffness in my back. I constantly felt the threat of the potential return of paralyzing bouts of pain running up and down my leg.

While I was striving to make my mark, prove myself to my father, and find myself as a person and as a professional, I was neglecting the most important relationships in my life. I was also destroying my own health in the process.

Then, courtesy of Jenifer, I had a painful but powerful epiphany that changed my life and my work.

Jenifer Robin Collins was born in her father's hometown—McGregor, Iowa—on November 9, 1961, exactly twelve days before I was born at Camden General Hospital in Camden, New Jersey, on November 21 of that same year. Of course, I have teased her from the beginning that she robbed the cradle.

Introduced by mutual friends, we have been inseparable from the day we met more than thirty-five years ago. Jen, Jeni, Jenny, or Jenifer, as she is variously known, fascinated me from day one. *She's a fighter*, I thought. At just five feet in height, she was then and is still today pound for pound the most courageous, outrageous, and contagious person I have ever known.

On the beach at the Jersey Shore one day while we were dating and admiring her lithe frame, I said, "You remind me of Bubba Smith," who was physically her total polar opposite.

Back in the 1970s, Bubba Smith was a massive defensive tackle for the Baltimore Colts NFL football team. While oddly humorous at the time, the nickname "Bubba" stuck. She has remained my Bubba ever since. The truth is, she has been every bit the fighter in life that the Hall of Fame tackle Bubba Smith was on the gridiron.

Should I have been surprised, then, to find that after a few years of marriage I would come racing in the back door of our quaint little Dutch colonial house in Paoli, Pennsylvania, excited to share the news of the big contract we'd just won, only to be greeted with a firm and direct, "Congrats, honey, now please take out the garbage." If there was a person born on this earth who, by sheer force of her will, could keep me from getting too big for my britches, it was Bubba.

For every victory, tragedy, breakthrough, or defeat, Bubba was there telling me to calm down, cut it out, get over it, and get on with it. She was also there to remind me that no matter how well Vertex did or what kind of aha moment I experienced that week, the garbage needed to go out, the kids needed to have their baths, and the dog needed to be fed.

One Friday after work, when we were talking in our kitchen, Bubba became the teacher of one of the greatest lessons I'd ever learned.

It was a beautiful fall day, and we'd had a great sales week at the company. I was characteristically fired up about it, and on the short drive home, I decided that it would be a perfect weekend for Jen and I to throw the camping gear, the dog, and the three kids—ages five, three, and one—into the jump seat of my Ford F-150 Super Cab pickup truck, for the scenic trek to Sullivan County and the Endless Mountains of Pennsylvania's Northern Tier.

"No way! We are not hopping in the truck and going to the mountains in fifteen minutes. Not happening." That was her first reply to my pitch.

I thought, *She's just not getting it. It's the perfect weekend to get out of here and go into the woods where the kids love to play. It would be relaxing and even a little romantic.* I upped the pressure a bit, making my case for why it would all go so well, confident that she would give in and we would have a wonderful time.

"Not happening." She was not budging. Not an inch.

There we were in our kitchen, which was a perfect square, like a boxing ring. Bubba was in one corner, by the little kitchen table. I was in the other corner, over by the stove. The chopping block I had gotten her for Christmas the year before sat squarely in the middle of the room, like a silent, patient referee.

Stalemated, I recalled Covey's encouragement from the *7 Habits*—that I should try to seek to understand before being understood, and that doing so required setting my own agenda aside and completely focusing on the moment from her point of view.

Heck, can't hurt, I thought. I took a deep breath, tried to set my enthusiasm for the trip aside, leaned across the chopping block, reducing the distance between us, and completely focused on her and what might be going on for her. She was making it abundantly clear that she had no interest in going away with me for the weekend, that it was too far and too much work, that I had been out of town most of the week, and the last thing she needed was a lot of extra work.

And then it happened. A thought entered my mind that came as a shock, *She is concerned about our children*. It was as though the chopping block had come to life as an actual referee, pushing me toward my corner counting 1, 2 . . . as I stumbled backward, dazed and confused as though struck by a right cross I never saw coming.

It had never dawned on me that underneath her protests was a simple and inarguably important concern: How are we going to just throw everything we need to care for three young children into a truck for a camping weekend with no prior plan, no food shopping, no packing, nothing? Who could argue with that?

The next thought that came into my consciousness was even more of a shock to me. *Oh my God, if I didn't understand Bubba today, how many times has she tried to get through to me and all I could think of was myself?*

The parade of epiphanies continued. *Oh no! If I've never understood my own wife, how many other people haven't I ever understood? What about their world, their lives, and their feelings? Ah! What about the company? What do people really think? What do they really need? Oh no!*

Eventually regaining some level of focus on Jen, I said, "Bubba, are you worried that we will not be able to take care of the kids on this trip? If so, I understand. We don't need to go."

She simply stared at me, mouth hanging slightly open, as if she'd just seen a ghost.

"It's about time you figured this out! Isn't it obvious that we can't just throw a weekend for three kids together in fifteen minutes?" she replied, a bit calmer now.

"As hard as it is to believe, no, it was not obvious to me. But it is now. I'm sorry." While I said this, I was wondering what else I didn't get and thinking, *I have to get to the office and find out what people really think.*

The change at Vertex began the Monday after I'd realized that I'd never really listened to Jen in order to understand any situation from her point of view. I went into the office that morning and started asking questions and truly listening to what people had to say. I focused on trying to understand their perspective, rather than on how I would form my response.

People were a bit shy at first. It must have reminded them of the scene in Charles Dickens's *A Christmas Carol* where Ebenezer Scrooge wakes up after having been visited by the three ghosts and is so happy to discover that it is still Christmas morning and that means he still has a chance to make his life right.

Before the chopping block epiphany, my goal every day was to cross items off my to-do list. A good day was when I got a lot of items crossed off and we had a good contract come in or we had a strong new sales month. That was it—that simple. How things got on the list almost did not matter. They were there, and they needed to get done.

Suddenly, here was a new me. I now seemed to have all the time in the world. I hung on every word each person had to say about their job, their thoughts about what we needed to do better, updates about their families—anything that really mattered to them.

I remember listening and looking at each person with wonder, as if at any moment I was about to discover a life-changing secret. And the discoveries flowed, one amazing realization after another. I was starting to live the change I had realized we needed to make as a company.

It was evident that our people were a virtual treasure trove of insight and knowledge. It was equally true that they had not been sharing that knowledge and insight with me or each other since it was not being sought out, encouraged, or appreciated.

Without knowing it, my conscious shock had triggered a cultural transformation for our small enterprise. From that moment when Jen and I faced off across the chopping block on a beautiful Friday afternoon, the effort to understand others' genuine motivations, at home and at work, became the journey of a lifetime.

REFLECTION

Looking back at the chopping block moment, I laugh at myself. Jen's resistance to my idea appears so obvious and understandable to me now. But back then, as self-assured, hyper, and headstrong as I was, it was a life-changing moment. The truth was that I had never truly tried to understand another person's angle!

My typical approach was to listen to others from my point of view and to judge their statements from the perspective of whether I was getting more or less of what I wanted. I was not often aware of what I wanted at the time, but I can now see that my life was a series of interactions designed to get more of what I wanted, even if what I wanted was to be helpful to others.

The problem was that I was being helpful to others to try and feel better about myself. I was doing it from my viewpoint rather than theirs. This proved to be not very helpful to them or to me.

I was expending massive amounts of effort to try and help people at work and my wife at home by giving them what I thought they wanted without ever asking them what that was. That habit changed profoundly in the days, weeks, months, and years after what I thought of as my chopping block epiphany. The realization that I had never truly understood Jen imprinted upon me that my way was only *one* way of viewing the world, not *the* way of viewing the world.

My chopping block epiphany was the first of many instances where an experience in my personal life challenged my worldview in ways that changed my approach to work. Over time I came to see that my work and my personal life were indivisible. Both spheres were creating experiences that would forever change who I was in every aspect of my life.

I wish I could say that at some point after my chopping block epiphany I managed to master the art of "seeking to understand," but the truth is that it remains a daily challenge. Almost always, if I seek to truly understand another person on their terms, I am amazed to discover a wholly different way of seeing the world.

Yet, even after all this time, seeking to understand other people remains a fascinating, frustrating, and fantastic journey. I have Jen to thank for sticking to her guns and challenging me to get outside of my self-centered cocoon.

ACTION STEPS—UNDERSTANDING THE OTHER POINT OF VIEW

Like the sensation of swimming, the act of seeking first to understand can't be conveyed in words. It has to be experienced.

Here is a simple way to experience the sensation of understanding another's point of view from their perspective.

1. Think of a friend, colleague, or family member whom you know well who disagrees with you about a matter of significant interest to them.

2. Ask them if they would be willing to help you understand their point of view and assure them that you're not trying to change their position or argue with them.

3. Set a dedicated time to have the conversation where you can have privacy and truly focus. This is not something to try in a busy restaurant or a ten-minute car ride. Ideally, you would be in person, or at least on Zoom, with plenty of time to talk.

4. Set a clear goal in your mind to let go of your own opinions or knowledge of the matter. Remind yourself that understanding the other's point of view is *not the same as agreeing with that point of view*. Let go of the urge to decide why you disagree and definitely let go of the need to argue. Just listen and try to understand.

5. Ask the individual to share their point of view on the subject, whatever it is. Listen with this simple question in mind: Why do they think and feel this way? Occasionally, share with the other person your understanding of what they're thinking and feeling. You can say, for example, "Do you mean X, and is that causing you to feel Y?"

6. When you're confident you understand both what the person thinks and what they feel about the matter, ask them, "Do you believe that I genuinely understand your views and how you feel about them?" Keep repeating back your understanding of what they are trying to convey until the other person says, "Yes, absolutely, you totally get it."

AI NOTE: It is essential to experience these action steps with other real people. Real people are a mix of thoughts, knowledge, beliefs, and feelings. Real people are rarely "logical." Often, feelings influence words and body language, making it difficult to truly understand others from their point of view. The only way to learn how to understand real people is to seek to understand real people.

CHAPTER 9

MY FATHER'S THERAPIST?

As a child, I lived in fear of my father. For as long as I could remember, I experienced him as something dangerous, unpredictable, and larger than life.

While I was never seriously harmed, discipline was administered with spankings, sometimes with the belt from his trousers. When my father was coming home from work, I learned to go into red alert mode, constantly scanning the environment for anything that might set him off.

There was never a time I can remember when my father and I had anything approaching a conversation or when he sought to understand my perspective about anything. I just accepted that sons don't have conversations with fathers; we do what we are told, and if we don't like it, we keep that to ourselves.

Typical of parents of his generation, he had no patience for any feeling from me but happy, OK, or "I'm sorry, it won't happen again." I learned to keep any expressions of fear, hurt, or joy to myself. Sharing those emotions had been met with stern reprisal, and I soon learned that it was much safer to simply swallow them or pretend that I never had any of those feelings in the first place.

Anger was specifically taboo. The only person free to be angry was my father. I firmly believed that if I were to show anger toward my father, I would be seriously harmed. Given how frightening and unfair I found his own anger, I quickly convinced myself that anger was bad and that, thankfully, I was never angry.

What my father and I did have was a bond around projects. We cut the grass together, raked the leaves together, worked on my model trains together, and even built a small wooden boat together. I looked forward to his arrival home after work, and I would often wait in the driveway hoping he had time to shoot some hoops, at the same time ever aware to gauge his mood before approaching him. And of course, we rooted for our sports teams together. We didn't talk about much, but we did do a lot.

By the time I was a teenager, my repression of all my feelings found expression in the same kind of rebellious behavior well-known to suburban teenage boys in the 1980s.

I consciously underperformed in school, maintaining a steady B-minus average while doing the absolute least work possible. I found a B-minus was the lowest I could go without risking life and limb at home. My friends and I drank illegally, drove while drinking, and tore mailboxes from their posts throughout the region, while also taking occasional overnight trips to the Jersey Shore with nowhere to stay but the car, the beach, or an occasional undisclosed use of my uncle's shore house.

Remarkably, my father seemed to treat all this rebellion as manly behavior, and I never got in any serious trouble for any of it. When I wound up as captain of the University of Richmond rugby club, he didn't say anything positive, but he didn't give me a hard time about it either.

Throughout that time, we never actually talked about anything meaningful, except for one time. Clearly put up to it by my mother, he asked me if I was being mindful about reproductive protection. That "conversation" lasted about fifteen seconds.

Dad: You're being careful about girls, right?

Me: Yeah.

Dad: Good.

It should have been no surprise, then, that when I agreed to come to work at the company, not only didn't we talk about it in advance, we also didn't talk about it when I was there either. He gave me a title and pretty much left me to my own devices.

So when I started to apply my learning from the chopping block experience, asking him questions and actually listening to him with real intent to understand what he was saying from his point of view, it was nothing short of a sea change in our relationship. Until that point, I had pretty much considered my father the protagonist in my life and the source of all that wasn't the way I wanted it to be.

Setting all my fears and resentments aside was a challenge, but it was essential if I was going to apply the Covey principles to our relationship. So I did, asking him open-ended questions and devoting my full attention to understanding his point of view.

Soon, my father was asking me to take long walks with him in the park near our office. We would walk in large circles around the baseball diamonds. He would talk about the business, his concerns, insights, assumptions, and challenges. My father said more words to me on each one of those walks than he had ever said to me in my entire life. When I could squeeze a word in, I would try to affirm my understanding of his perspective and how he felt about whatever the issue was.

On one occasion, perhaps after the fifth or sixth of these walks, he shared so much angst and frustration that I was genuinely frightened, for him and for me. I couldn't wait to get back into my office. When I finally did get there, I quickly shut the door, grabbed the phone, and called Jim.

"Hello."

"Jim, it's Jeff. I think I am my father's therapist." And tears flowed like they hadn't in as long a time as I could remember.

It was then Jim's turn to play therapist, helping me put my father's need to share in perspective. He helped me understand that in my father's life, growing up in a strict German home in the 1940s and '50s, he had likely never been genuinely listened to until these walks, and that it was a great gift for me to be trusted with his innermost fears and doubts.

REFLECTION

Jim was certainly right. Today I can't imagine how my father would ever have been in a situation where anyone had actually listened to him with an intent to understand him without judgment. No doubt my mother did all she could, but I suspect that the nature of the gender roles they were both raised within likely limited the level of vulnerability that was possible between them.

Of course, I was no therapist and had only entered therapy myself that same year. While it definitely wasn't therapy, I had, without realizing it, created the safest place for my father to express himself that he, or I, had ever experienced.

What unfolded was remarkable. Throughout my entire life I had wished my father was a different, gentler, and less frightening person. Thanks to Covey and Jim Patton, what I experienced during those walks was someone trying desperately to be the person he thought he was supposed to be—strong, silent, solitary, competitive, decisive, and domineering. Yet at the same time, he had been feeling completely uncertain of himself, his inclinations, and his abilities.

For the first time in my life, my father became a real person rather than a mythic, terrifying figure to be avoided and manipulated. Rather than trying to change him, I had changed myself by trying to understand and appreciate him. And remarkably, once I stopped wishing he would change, he became more trusting, less demanding, and more accessible.

It was a few decades later as he was declining into dementia before my father ever said, "I am proud of you" or "I love you." Nevertheless, we became closer than we had ever been before and certainly more than I had ever believed possible. All thanks to a book, a mentor, and an aha moment across a chopping block.

As my father's dementia progressed, I found myself increasingly appreciative of what he had done for me. With the added benefit of hindsight, I could now see that part of his offer to have me join the company was his adherence to old European ideas of primogeniture, where the oldest son assumes the responsibilities of the father, but also that he could see (and my mother no doubt could see) that I was in trouble in my late twenties and that I needed some stability in my life.

I sat down with him when he could still understand what I was saying and thanked him explicitly for all he had done to help me make it to and through adulthood. It was probably our longest and most intimate conversation ever. I did almost all of the talking, and all he said was, "You're welcome. Let's go play pool." But it was evident that he heard me and understood the earnestness of my appreciation.

When my father passed, the reflection I shared at his memorial service was that we did projects together, and our time at Vertex was our biggest project. And, like the boat we built together, I tried to finish the things he had started.

ACTION STEPS: EMPATHIC LISTENING FOR THOSE CLOSEST TO YOU

It's one thing to strive to understand a peer at work. It's another thing to strive to understand an important person in your life, perhaps your supervisor, a parent, loved one, or close friend. These relationships are more complex because we are more invested in them. We have more at stake, and so does the other person. There can be significant past experiences with the individual that add an element of emotional risk in the relationship, making the listening experience more challenging . . . and more valuable.

In the case of my father, there were lifelong experiences that literally shaped who I was and how I viewed the world. He was also my boss, shaping my future in ways that I couldn't fully understand. After Jenifer and my mother, the relationship with my father meant more to who I saw myself as, and who I would become, than any other person.

The most important thing to remember is that there is a massive difference between learning how to truly listen and appreciate another person's perspective and providing therapy. While at age twenty-nine I may have thought that I was being my father's therapist because he was sharing real feelings with me for the first time, I had no idea what being a therapist actually entailed.

Now that I know, I have to emphasize that these action steps are not even remotely therapy. They are simple steps anyone can take to build an understanding of another person from that individual's viewpoint and are intended as a practical introduction to a way of continuously building lifelong relationships.

1. Check in with yourself. Do you really and truly want to understand an important person better, or are you hoping to get something in return for your attention to their point of view? If you are trying to get something in return, counsel yourself to set that desire aside for the purpose of this experience. Do not attempt the following steps until you can honestly say that you are genuinely seeking to understand the other person.

2. Is the other person willing to participate, or will that person feel as though you are experimenting on them or manipulating

them with your questions? Check in with the person you want to understand better with a simple question: "I want to understand your views better. Do you mind if I ask you some questions and test my understanding with you, so I am sure that I genuinely appreciate your perspective?" If the individual is OK with that, then great. If not, thank them and perhaps try again a few months later.

3. You could ask many open-ended questions. It's important that you ask questions for which you don't already have your own answer or position defined. You may consider three simple questions:

    a. You have expressed interest in the past on (subject here). Can you share with me why this subject is of interest to you?

    b. Do you have a hope or aspiration regarding (this subject)? Ideally, what do you wish would happen?

    c. How do you feel about (this subject)? Is it personally important to you? Why is that?

4. Reflect on your understanding of the subject from the point of view of the individual you are interviewing. You might say, "What I am understanding is that (this subject) interests you because (their rationale here) and you wish that eventually (their aspiration here) would happen. I hear you saying that you feel strongly about this because (their meaning here)."

5. Confirm your understanding: "Do you feel that I genuinely understand your views on this subject?" If the individual says yes, thank the individual. If they say no or they continue talking, likely filling in gaps where they might not have been clear or felt understood, patiently repeat steps 4 and 5 until the individual tells you "Yes, you get it."

Resist the temptation to complete the preceding cycle and then launch into your own views on the matter. It is important for the "understanding" to stand on its own. Only express your views if the other person asks you for them with a genuine desire to understand on their part. Otherwise, your desire to be understood will undermine their sense of having been understood. You can approach the person later and ask them if they would like to know how you feel about the topic.

AI NOTE: As with the action steps in chapter 8, this experience can only be had with another real person.

CHAPTER 10

IN LIVING COLOR

It was a stunning fall day, and I was driving home alone through the Endless Mountains of Northeastern Pennsylvania on my way back from Sullivan County. I had just finished a satisfying weekend visioning retreat at Eagles Mere with a group of about twenty-five employees from all parts of the company.

We were making progress toward creating a vision of the future of the company. The excitement and curiosity of the people on this retreat were palpable. Away from our day-to-day responsibilities, we had the freedom to explore, poke, and prod around the question of what kind of future we wanted to create. I kept myself in check and tried to facilitate (and not sway) the discussions. It was a total win, and I was proud of what we had accomplished that day as the retreat came to a close.

After saying goodbye to everyone, I hopped into my truck and started driving home on the mountain roads, admiring the spectacular fall foliage on a positively sparkling day. As I drove, I pondered the experience that had just unfolded. I found myself thinking seriously for the first time about my own future and what I might want that future to be.

After about forty-five minutes on the road, deep in self-reflection and appreciation of the natural beauty that surrounded me, I suddenly became transfixed. I was awestruck with the awareness that I felt deeply connected to everything I saw spread out before me.

It was as though I was lifted from my truck seat and spread out, like a beam of light, to touch every leaf, blade of grass, and cloud in the sky. I was overcome with a profound sense of peace and of knowing that somehow, someway, everything served everything else and that I was deeply and inextricably one with it all.

Nothing seemed fixed in place or time or stuck in any way. Everything appeared infused with a boundless sense of potential. I suddenly knew that the possibility of infinite potential was everywhere around me. It was not so much that I was connected to what I saw, but that I felt completely indivisible from what I was experiencing.

A few minutes after having this profound experience, another mind-blowing awareness came over me. I realized that Vertex was far more important to the world than its apparent role as merely a tax software company. It, too, was connected and an indivisible part of everything else, and it had a purpose far beyond what I had previously imagined.

Sorting through what had just happened to me while trying to keep my truck on the road, my simple insight slowly became clearer. Although we developed tax software for clients like Apple, Microsoft, Nestlé, Ford, and thousands of others, we really existed so *they* could make better computers, software, food products, vehicles, and so on. When our customers made great products, this made life on earth better for *everyone* in ways that were sometimes life-enabling, sometimes lifesaving, and sometimes crucial to the very fabric of our way of life.

I began to see that the quality of our human existence was impacted significantly by the businesses that provide us with food, water, shelter, light, energy, health care, security, communications, and entertainment. What had been mere intellectual knowledge had been transformed into a deeply visceral understanding.

Every facet of our human experience in the developed world is influenced by the array of goods and services provided by the corporations we rely upon and contribute to. We find meaning in safety, connection, knowledge, nourishment, and well-being. And, whether we are actively aware of it or not, it is corporations that bring us the goods and services that enable us to more fully realize a good bit of the meaning we need and seek from life.

After all, nothing is more meaningful than the food we eat, and it has been a long time since most of us were farmers, living off the land. Today, given how separated we are from the sources of our nourishment, without the supply chains of for-profit enterprises, millions upon millions of us would starve. And yet, all the for-profit companies that make that food supply possible, and all of their employees, are constantly told that their primary purpose is profit for shareholders.

Corporations, including our customers, partners, suppliers, and competitors, have become indispensable to human social activity, safety, wellness, longevity, and prosperity. They have contributed mightily to a dramatic gain in both length of human life expectancy and quality of life enjoyment. I could now see that these corporations held keys critical to unlocking the promise of human dignity and prosperity for humanity. It was all one thing, infused with incredible potential for positive impact.

I also realized that to have a meaningful career you did not have to work for a nonprofit organization like Amnesty International, the American Red Cross, or a St. Jude Medical Center, as important and rewarding as those careers can be. With profound clarity, I realized that I was in a position to make a major impact on society through our work at the company. And the same was true for others, whether they chose careers in computer programming at IBM, on the assembly line at Ford, or in any other profession or company that contributed to something that society needed. It all mattered more than I ever realized.

Meaning was there all along, right in front of me, and all I had to do was shift my point of view. It was my big bang moment. My life and career would never be the same. From that point on, everything I did emanated from an entirely different perspective and a newfound sense of transcendent purpose.

REFLECTION

To say that this experience transformed my high-energy passion to do good into some kind of obsessive missionary zeal would be an understatement. From that moment on I could not see a monthly quota, strategic plan, or accounting statement as anything more than a means to a much larger vision—a transcendent sense that Vertex existed to serve a massive purpose for the betterment of humanity.

This new insight helped me better understand the importance of financial performance. I now could see that without strong financial performance, the company couldn't fund the investments necessary to make the larger positive impact to society that was possible through advanced tax technology.

My former sense that we had to generate growth and profit to meet the expectations of shareholders and employees was true but didn't address the larger purpose of the business itself. I could now see how it was all deeply interconnected in a self-reinforcing cycle of positive impact.

Talented people, properly compensated by visionary investors, created better technology that could improve the performance of our clients' enterprises, allowing them to put more time, effort, and money into improving their service to humanity in the form of nourishment, information, shelter, medical care, security, and all manner of basic human needs. The better we did, the better our customers did, the better off society was, and that in turn increased sales and profits, which were shared with our people and investors. It was a virtuous cycle anchored in social benefit. In that moment, I knew that nearly every for-profit company was actually a for-purpose enterprise, whether they knew it or not.

But my new insight, in 1992, created a quandary. While I saw the company as part of the very fabric of society and a key part of the essential infrastructure for long-term global prosperity, my colleagues saw a promising business that needed to meet the immediate expectations of its customers, owners, and employees, and not much else beyond that. All very typical and reasonable expectations.

Jim clearly had experienced the "oneness" that I had experienced. That explained a lot about the way he was mentoring me. He remained a remarkable source of support as I tried to navigate a world that I now saw as operating in black and white while I believed I could see everything in living color.

Never again could I hear the term "agriculture industry" and not think that the very term takes the meaning out of "nourishing humanity," which is the purpose agriculture actually serves. Supply chains became "meaning" chains in my new understanding of how all of our efforts ultimately supported all of what we rely on for the lives we live.

During the Covid pandemic, I took extra time to thank the person at the grocery checkout for "making it possible for me to have food to eat today." When I was recently hospitalized, I made a point to express gratitude to the cleaning people who came to my room every day, letting them know that "without you, the doctors can't save lives."

So yes, full disclosure, I am a bit obsessive about recognizing the contributions of every single person who helps put food on the table, cars on the road, and news on my phone.

Yet the world operates on the premise that business exists for the primary purpose of making money for the shareholder and that all workers work for the primary purpose of making a paycheck.

But tell that to the person on the operating table waiting for a liver transplant, who would have no hope of survival without the thousands of supposedly for-profit businesses that contribute all the products and services that are essential to making their surgery a success. From the scalpel manufacturer to the builders who built the hospital and the tools used by the people who clean the floors, everything in that operating room was made possible by people working in businesses. Without them, the liver transplant patient would not have a snowball's chance in hell of living another day.

ACTION STEPS—CONNECTING TO A HIGHER PURPOSE

The importance of what you contribute to the world through your work is undeniable; however, if you are like I was in 1992, you might not realize the larger benefit of your efforts.

Try these simple questions to begin peeling back the layers of meaning already available to you.

1. What do you do?

2. How does what you do contribute to what your company (or household or nonprofit) does?

3. What does the company, household, or nonprofit do?

4. How does your company contribute to fulfilling the needs of its customers, whether they are people or other businesses?

5. Now, imagine all the companies, households, or nonprofits that do what yours does and all the people and organizations who receive the benefit of all of those efforts. For example, if you stock shelves with produce at the grocery store, imagine all of the people stocking shelves in all the grocery stores in the world serving all the people buying food.

6. Thinking about that bigger benefit, how is society as a whole impacted by it? What would the impact be if no one did what you do? For example, during the pandemic, if people hadn't gone to the grocery stores and stocked the shelves, we wouldn't have had access to any fresh food (unless you are a farmer and grow it yourself!).

AI NOTE: Artificial intelligence can be enormously helpful as you consider how your contribution to your workplace contributes to your customers and how their work contributes to their customers and so on. Be prepared to be surprised by how much impact you may be having that you might not have realized before!

CHAPTER 11

THE MIRACLE MACHINE

While the visioning process that started in Eagles Mere became a cornerstone of the new Vertex culture, there was more we could do to instill creativity and meaning into the day-to-day interactions at Vertex and support the desired growth we were pursuing.

I began to realize that while meaning is, at its core, wholly individual in interpretation, a group setting can lead to an explosion of ideas, perspectives, and solutions that in and of itself creates meaning for the team and its individual members.

People process things differently and come at problems and issues from different perspectives. I could see that clearly now. But how do you build a culture of creativity within a tax software company dominated by subject matter experts who were born-and-bred analytical problem solvers?

The essence of creativity is the art of seeing things differently. With creativity, insights often emerge that lead to great breakthroughs. I had seen it applied in the arts and even in the hospitality business. But in our typically numbers-driven, business-to-business environment, who are the artists and how do they thrive?

Starting with the leadership team, I instilled a team-oriented approach consisting of the various departmental leaders. Our approach was process-driven and highly collaborative, and we strived for consensus-based decision-making, which certainly was not the norm at the time.

Not surprisingly, we ran into some obstacles—including how much the members of the team sought to influence me, given my role as CEO, or take their cue from what I had to say in our meetings. I realized quickly this was not the recipe I had in mind that would lead to breakthrough thinking. These habits needed to be addressed.

With Jim's coaching outside the room, I started offering fewer of my own views. I began to hold open the space, a very painful space, where members of the team wouldn't get a signal from me as to where I might have been leaning on whatever issue we were attempting to tackle.

The truth was, I did not know where we would come out because I was learning as much as or more than anyone in the room. Even though I had the most formal authority, I had the least amount of experience and even less real knowledge and expertise about the tax and technology topics that drove the business.

Time and again, I found myself shocked by what I learned in those meetings. Eventually, I became aware that others were having the same experience, whether they wanted to openly admit it or not. In the end, however, we too often found ourselves locked in what felt like mortal combat trying to make decisions. I was not sure why or what to do to get us out of the deadlocks.

Learning how to collaborate was not as easy as the management books made it appear. We mostly just battled our way to some begrudging agreements. Everyone would leave the meeting room feeling mentally bruised and battered.

After about a year, we engaged Jim to help us create a better way. He said, "Well, you could start applying the Rule of Three." None of us had a clue what Jim was talking about, but as we sat dumbfounded, he began to cue up our next life-changing experience.

Jim shared that in our quest to make decisions we were focused on debating the obvious pros and cons of the topic. Framing the discussion in this manner naturally sets up a win-or-lose situation—a right or wrong way of looking at the issue.

The Rule of Three is a simple model to avoid this trap. It suggests there are three points of view: (1) **Advocation**—those promoting a certain solution, (2) **Restraint**—those who are pushing back on the idea, and (3) **Reconciliation**—those who come up with a completely new solution that the team can support and is satisfying to both advocating and restraining parties.

Advocation and restraint tend to work like opposite poles of a magnet, and we were getting stuck without a way to reconcile these often-contentious discussions. While the gentle reframing of the notions of pro and con, win or lose, was super helpful, the real secret sauce was the concept of the reconciling force.

Jim explained that the reconciling force is influenced heavily by the state of being of the collaborators. We were baffled by the term. Jim explained that it had two basic dimensions: (1) how our feelings and beliefs helped shape our perspective and (2) how our interpretation of the purpose of what we were discussing impacted our perspective.

For example, coming into a meeting, was our state of being combative, open-minded, or understanding? Or were we simply checked out? Was it our intent to do what is best for ourselves, our employees, our departments, the company, our customers, or the industry as a whole?

Up to this point we approached these sessions as a debate. It was either a good idea or a bad idea, and we generally took sides in predictable ways. It had never dawned on us that we were in a pattern that had more to do with our roles or the way we perceived each other rather than the actual merits of the matter centered on a higher purpose.

If the idea held the promise of achieving more sales more quickly, Sales and Marketing were for it. If the idea was about investing in capacity and infrastructure, Software Development and Customer Service were for it.

The battle lines were often drawn between those who saw themselves as primarily responsible for the revenue and those who saw themselves as primarily responsible for the customer satisfaction side of the business.

Jim wisely suggested that as a reconciling principle we start asking ourselves, "What's best for the entire organization over time?" He also suggested that we continue paying more attention to our empathic listening skills and learning to deeply respect each other's views as we worked to make decisions.

Over time something remarkable started to happen. And then it kept happening. We reached the point where we knew that if we stuck with any issue, it would happen. The *it* was the emergence of a new and creative solution to whatever the problem was. The solutions felt like they came out of nowhere and from outside the awareness of any of those present at the start of the dialogue.

By regularly applying the Rule of Three, we started to genuinely trust that our collaborative approach would yield results beyond our initial expectations. Typically, we would spend the first third of a meeting sharing perspectives and striving to understand each other's views.

We would then have this weird middle time where it was evident that neither the advocating idea nor the restraining view represented a complete solution. That recognition led to a growing sense that there was something meaningful to be developed from the dialogue.

This awareness was often followed by a painful stretch where it was obvious that an answer was needed but the proposals on the table were nonstarters. The tension in the room was frequently unbearable, as minutes and even hours would pass as the group would search for a thread, opening, or nugget of inspiration.

And then someone would offer an idea. And then others, sensing its potential, would build on it further. We kept building until we reached the point where, to our astonishment, we had this entirely new solution that none of us could have predicted going in—one that was so much better than we could have ever thought possible!

The essence of what we discovered is that we could create a new understanding, previously unappreciated by any of us. This transformed our exchanges from debates, power plays, and passive-aggressive manipulation to a genuine appreciation for each other's perspectives and a belief that together we would work through these issues to a new creative solution.

The simple Rule of Three that Jim Patton taught us was like Stephen Covey's seeking to understand to the third power. I call it the Miracle Machine because many of the creative solutions we came to felt like miracles to all of us.

Often, the best answer was not known to any of us before we entered the dialogue. After some time, we came to realize that it almost did not make sense to try and come to an answer without the full group, as we knew we would realize better answers together than we could alone.

These experiences changed me deeply, and they changed others on our leadership team as well. The spouse of one of our executives approached me at a company social and said, "I do not know what you are doing, but my spouse is a better person because of it. Thank you!"

REFLECTION

These lengthy dialogues at work were building a foundation, not only for our culture, but for our lives. Seeing the value of the Rule of Three in action, I began to apply this approach in all my relationships—at work, at home, socially, and in the community.

Of course, in the office with the help of a sophisticated facilitator, I was in an ideal environment to develop these skills and see their benefits. Like most people, my family was not interested in being roped into some formal process for "creating shared meaning."

What I had to learn to do with respect for all involved was to simply seek to understand until we arrived at an outcome we could all feel was a better option. And, over decades of application, I have seen patterns emerge that make it easier to forge shared solutions.

For example, Jen is much more attuned and capable when it comes to logistics than I am. Having entered filmmaking after our youngest was off to college, she often says, "I've been a producer my entire life." With entrepreneurial parents, she had worked at everything from pumping gas and cleaning motel rooms to waiting tables. She will instantly see the complexity involved in getting anything done.

She will also cut right through to the essence of an issue, like an eagle targeting its prey. I am more likely to see the big picture and imagine entirely different approaches, even different visions, than we had when we entered a given conversation.

Our whole approach to making decisions has evolved naturally toward a dance of why and how, and often we trade roles. Now, Jen sometimes offers a bigger picture insight that changes the whole context, and I occasionally offer concerns about how something will work logistically.

The one constant is we assume positive intent and value the other person's perspective. This is important because experience has taught me that no two people see a situation entirely the same way. No matter the situation, meaning is in the eye of the beholder. Another person's meaning is often quite different from mine and is influenced by that individual's knowledge, experience, and beliefs.

Thirty years after Jim introduced us to the Rule of Three, it continues to be the source of remarkable insight and appreciation for others. It continues to help me achieve a deeper meaning and fulfillment in my work life relationships.

ACTION STEPS—CREATING A RECONCILING SOLUTION

Since the Rule of Three is built on the foundation of seeking to understand and requires diverse participants with real, not made up, concerns, here is a straightforward approach to creating an experience of the Miracle Machine for yourself.

1. Pick a topic or issue that requires a solution. It can be anything.

2. Engage a friend, spouse, or colleague to come up with solutions to discuss, making sure they are different from the solutions you have already considered.

3. After a "seek to understand" dialogue, capture the key points behind both the advocation and restraints of each position.

4. Then discuss what could be a creative third solution rather than a winner and loser.

5. After you achieve a plausible creative solution, discuss how this experience of seeking a reconciling creative solution was different than your typical experience of problem-solving with others.

AI NOTE: Many group decisions suffer from assumptions and beliefs about certain facts or data that cannot be easily accessed. AI presents an incredible opportunity to deal in facts rather than speculation; this can greatly enhance collaboration. It can also help rapidly model different plausible scenarios, identifying risks and many other ways of improving group decision-making. What AI cannot do is create actual understanding and shared commitment in the people who need to agree in order to commit the organization to a decision. That process remains messy, complicated by myriad human factors. AI cannot replace human collaboration.

CHAPTER 12

AN EVEN BIGGER GIFT

"**Y**ou can think of your child's autism as a gift," said the counselor at the treatment center.

Those are hard words to hear when your oldest son has seemingly disappeared before your eyes, and you are feeling helpless to do anything about it and guilty over what you might have done to cause it. And now these people are suggesting, in the most compassionate way possible, that our son Kyle's autism is somehow a gift!

At first, I resisted going there. But as I held a photograph of Kyle, then five, I started crying, thinking about how true that was and what a gift he had been to us in our lives. And maybe his incomprehensible behavior held clues to a new understanding of what it means to be human, to truly love another person, and to be deeply committed to their journey, whatever that journey may be.

That was the beginning of a process that ultimately enabled our son to emerge from severe autism into normal adulthood and for me to discover a whole world of new insights about myself. It turned out to be one of the most meaningful and important moments of my life.

To create the best possible environment for Kyle to grow, I needed first to think about my feelings, attitudes, and beliefs about him, about autism, and about parenting. What I learned was that I could change those beliefs, attitudes, and feelings and in so doing, I could make a profound difference in my growth and my son's.

Of course, I was not aware of any of that at the time. And that is why the process that we were introduced to was so powerful. We knew that we loved and cared about our son and wanted him to have a full experience of life.

But Kyle was unwilling to engage with us, his siblings, or other children. He was comfortable in his own world—flipping and spinning anything he could get his hands on and hiding under blankets for hours at a time.

He exhibited no meaningful language, no eye contact, no interaction. I would throw a ball to him, and it would just bounce off his body, with no effort on his part to even attempt to catch it, even though I knew he was physically capable of doing so.

The facilitators at the treatment center* where we learned a unique approach to living with autism would invite me to reflect on my experience with our son.

What followed was a thoughtful unpacking of a recent experience I may have had with him, how I felt about the experience, why I felt the way I did, and ultimately what I was believing about Kyle and myself that may have led me to feel the way I did.

It was a fascinating journey through myriad and intertwined assumptions, beliefs, and attitudes that I had accumulated over the years and how they shaped my reactions to Kyle's behavior.

After years of self-reflection I came to understand that my feelings didn't need to be automatic reactions to what was happening around me. I realized that just because other people might feel a certain way about a certain event in their lives, I didn't have to feel the same way when confronted by a similar situation.

---

* We followed the program offered by the Autism Treatment Center of America.

Not only did this experience lead me to completely change how I feel about rainy days, it also totally transformed how I felt about Kyle's autism. It was as if I was reading a book about my own evolution, never having opened the pages before. The experience taught me that I could be content with our son, and myself, even if he were deep into one of his most autistic cycles.

My experience was that while my automatic response was often frustration and self-blame, I learned to see it coming, remind myself that I did not need to blame myself, and that being frustrated was not going to help Kyle at all. In fact, it would do just the opposite.

Over a span of about five years, we worked with our son in his dedicated playroom, with Jenifer training and managing a staff of remarkable volunteers to have someone working with him all day, every day, seven days a week. It was a slow process, but eventually Kyle transformed and came out of his shell. I am deeply grateful to everyone who contributed to his development.

Those five years coincided directly with the late 1990s period when we were steadily transforming the company around the principles of collaboration. I realized that scenarios at work virtually mirrored what was happening in Kyle's autism playroom. Given the diverse talents at Vertex, creating an environment where people could forge a shared understanding and commitment around complex challenges was not dissimilar to trying to decode the communication challenges faced by our autistic son. It was like cultivating a garden hoping it would grow and flourish. I was becoming a gardener at home and at work.

REFLECTION

Thanks to Kyle's program, I was able to gain a level of insight about the beliefs I was unconsciously carrying around about myself, others, and the work we do. I was also learning that to truly seek to understand I had to completely set aside my assumptions about any of our technical domains and the unique people who specialized in them and do what I could to join them in their respective worlds.

This awareness led me to view others' behavior from a much more empathic viewpoint. After I realized that I had no clue about my own layers of beliefs and attitudes that were shaping my reactions to external events, I became better able to appreciate the depth of complexity lying beneath behavior in others that I found confusing.

Previously I could only wonder what layers of beliefs and attitudes operated beneath their choices. Our journey with Kyle's autism at home served to deepen my commitment to creating an environment at work where people could get in touch with what they really cared about, engaging with a purpose energized by a deep sense of self-awareness, of intrinsic meaning, as well as the beliefs upon which that meaning was founded.

ACTION STEPS—BECOMING MEANING AWARE

In the 1980s there was a well-known iterative problem-solving method known as The Five Whys where you take a problem statement and repeatedly ask, "Why did this problem occur?" to unearth the root cause.

While the technique is meant to be challenging, it offers an unbiased, open-ended invitation to consider the motivations and meaning behind our choices. Your *why* in support of any choice is often supported by other *whys*, which we hold so deeply that we do not even know they are there.

The Five Whys is powerful. Developed by Toyota, the technique involves asking "why" five or more times to determine a root cause from a group of symptoms. By asking *why* multiple times, the final goal is to reach the fix that has the flaws worked out of it. Each why is based on the answer to the previous why question. Eventually the questioner whittles down and identifies the core issue.

The Five Whys is intended to help peel back the layers of intrinsic meaning that inform the choices we make in our work lives. Let's try it.

1. Consider an important choice you have made recently that impacted your work life. It could be something big, like quitting your job, or much smaller, like stepping up to take a new assignment.

2. Thinking about that decision, in a quiet reflective space, on a walk, or sitting in a park, ask yourself, "Why did I make that decision?"

3. After taking some minutes to reflect on your rationale, your why, ask yourself a deeper question about the reason you just gave yourself: "Why did I think what I thought that led me to make that decision?"

4. What insights emerge for you about why you made the decision and why you thought your reasons were the right ones? Now, consider those reasons supporting your rationale and consider that there is a why underneath them. What are those *whys*?

5. Make some notes and call a friend who is willing to help you with seeking to understand and the Rule of Three. Ask them if you can share your ideas with them and invite them to ask you to go further.

AI NOTE: AI is not recommended as an aid in this experience, as it can interfere with you developing your own self-awareness.

CHAPTER 13

IN SEARCH OF THE ETERNAL BUZZ

Being the life of the party had been a big part of my cherished self-image. In college I was voted "Most Likely to Be Seen at Barry's," which was a popular watering hole near the University of Richmond. I even had a bumper sticker on my car that read, "Get Drunk and BE SOMEBODY."

My other favorite bumper sticker was "In Search of the Eternal Buzz." I thought I had been on a journey to find the eternal buzz, only to realize that there was a much more profound buzz and that it was far more eternal than I could have ever imagined.

After my "in living color" experience in the Endless Mountains of Pennsylvania and the revelation that everything was actually part of one thing, I knew my life needed to change. I quickly concluded that my pattern of obsessive work followed by obsessive partying was getting in the way of fully experiencing my newfound awareness.

Afraid to lose this sense of connectedness, I resolved to step off the partying treadmill and step up onto the wagon in the hope of freeing myself from feeling the constant tug of "go, go, go" at all times of the day and night.

After my revelation, my search for the eternal buzz came to a screeching halt and a new search was launched, this time without the beer goggles. I had no idea how hard it would be to hold on to the transcendent mindset I had glimpsed on that beautiful fall day, but I knew that booze was not the doorway to "BE SOMEBODY" I once believed it to be. As much as I loved a good time, I could see how my excessive drinking was getting in the way of my ability to stay connected to my newly discovered awareness.

One Saturday, Jen arrived home toting a case of beer. I looked at her and said, "I'm not drinking." Not for a second did I consider what this announcement might mean to her or anyone else.

As with so many of my other personal and professional decisions, I had followed my father's behavioral pattern and failed to discuss a major life decision with the person (or people) who would be most affected by it. I simply announced to Jen that I was quitting drinking.

She was skeptical, and for good reason. She had no idea about what was going on inside me—because I hadn't shared it with her—and I had no idea how to explain it to her. Even Jim Patton was skeptical, asking, "Do you have the support you need?" when I informed him that I was not drinking.

Having no idea what Jim might be talking about (as usual), I simply carried on. The seven years between my thirty-third and fortieth years were a mixture of a new kind of freedom and sense of being that I found deeply fulfilling. But it was also a terribly lonely space where I felt isolated and unable to connect with others, estranged by the change that had occurred within me that led to my dramatic outward shift.

Prior to my decision to stop drinking, I had been living a double life for as long as I could remember.

On the outside, I was the happy family man and a driven but

caring business leader. On the inside, I resented what I felt was a lack of appreciation for who I really was, and I repressed that simmering but unconscious resentment with a steady stream of overscheduled activities and the alcohol that went with them. It is no wonder "Behind Blue Eyes" by The Who was one of my favorite songs. It perfectly describes the angst and repressed rage that I believed no one else could understand.

I didn't think for a second that I was or could become an alcoholic. After all, I didn't live under a bridge, wear a large coat dug out of a dumpster, and drink out of a paper bag. I didn't need rehab to quit or meetings to stay sober.

Jim was incredibly supportive, as were the people who helped us with Kyle's autism. Nevertheless, I still felt oddly connected to all and everything at a spiritual level even while I felt disconnected from the people I was engaged with at a business, social, or emotional level.

REFLECTION

During those seven years, Vertex enjoyed remarkable business success. Our efforts to evolve the organization to be more flexible, humane, agile, and responsive to the meaning of our work were making a real difference.

And yet, the bigger dream of making a major impact through the work we did and showing the way to a new kind of humane organization in the way we worked together seemed to move further away as we grew closer to it.

Why? I didn't know. I felt like an enigma wrapped up in a conundrum, both special and worthless at the same time, but now with a North Star shining its light on a path ahead that I did not fully understand but had to follow. There was no going back.

When my father asked me to join his company and my knee-jerk response, without any discussion, was "OK," I had made a completely reactive decision that shaped the future of my work life. This situation was completely different.

When I had a personal revelation that everything was connected and decided to stop drinking so I could better understand what that was all about, I was making a conscious choice to move toward what I thought was a better way of being and working.

Previously the North Star of my work life had been to prove something to my father. My new North Star was to be of service to the greater good through my work in business and my own hoped-for development. The decision to stop drinking helped me better focus on this newfound sense of purpose and be more present with those around me who would come together to create the future, just as we had imagined we would at our Endless Mountains retreat.

I felt an uneasy sense of progress while still getting comfortable with all of the changes I was experiencing.

ACTION STEPS—DISCOVERING YOUR NORTH STAR

I have come to understand, decades later, that these kinds of changes happen for people all the time. Nevertheless, a transformative revelation is not required to decide that it is time for a change in one's work life. Furthermore, sometimes a change in someone else's work life creates a demand for change in one's own work life, like when a significant other loses their job or when a family member requires significant care.

There is no right or wrong answer when it comes to defining your work life North Star, but it sure does help if you know what it is! Here are some simple steps to develop a sense of your own North Star.

1. Drawing upon your reflections from The Five Whys exercise in chapter 12, identify the North Star that is guiding your

work life today. It may help to reflect on what you may have thought your North Star was when you first entered the workforce. How has your North Star changed since then?

2. To help stretch your thinking and imagination, consider how you might feel ten years after your retirement. Imagine yourself reflecting on your career with the perspective of a seventy-five-year-old, looking back and taking stock. What do you hope the sum of your work will have meant to you when all is said and done?

3. Now consider the path you will follow from where you are to your seventy-five-year-old future self. Describe the North Star, or guiding aspiration, that you will follow on your journey.

AI NOTE: As in your work to imagine your dream work life, AI can be helpful in expressing your seventy-five-year-old future self and your guiding aspiration. You may want to simply talk freely to an AI about what you might imagine you want to feel and who you want to be at seventy-five, asking the AI to help you express your ideas succinctly and compellingly in words that sound like you. AI is amazingly talented at doing such exercises. You may want to go further and ask AI for ideas about what you may want to consider if you were to draw a winding path from where you are to where you are wanting to arrive, legacy firmly established. (I wish I'd had AI when I was thirty!)

ARE WE THERE YET?

The early phases of my career were consumed by what I will call a period of searching, followed by a period of discovery, and then a time of relative stability, applying what had been revealed.

Taken as a whole, one could say that I was exploring new possibilities and testing those new possibilities in the real world of work and life, for the first time sensing the inextricable connection of the two formerly separate spheres.

The experience was deeply affirming. The insights from my period of exploration fueled a transformation in the way I thought and felt about work, leading to a change in my behavior at work and at home. These changes elicited adjustments in my relationships and fueled my ongoing development.

I was exploring a new way of being in a concept of a work life that I couldn't have even conceived of when I first entered the workforce. The entire process was both challenging and rewarding.

From the perspective of my mid-sixties, looking back at this significant phase of my work life, I can see that the biggest lesson is that I wasn't nearly as enlightened by my discoveries as I thought I was.

As it turned out, the ego—my "original programming"—was a formidable foe. During this initial phase of exploration, I actually believed that I had all the wisdom I needed and couldn't see how my insecurities and unexamined beliefs continued to shape my attitude toward the experience I was having. I mistook a little bit of growth for all the growth I would need, and that false assumption left me vulnerable to new challenges.

Ultimately, I learned that there is no peak to the mountain of personal growth. Today I continue to have experiences that remind me that there is always more to learn, more growth to gain, and more opportunity to develop an even more meaningful work life than I ever thought possible.

UNDERSTANDING

A 100 PERCENT MORE MEANINGFUL WORK LIFE

After my big bang moment, my quest to find meaning and connect the dots continued both at home and at the office. Soon I could see more clearly how activities at work and home, generally considered to be separate and divisible from each other, were much more deeply connected than they appeared on the surface.

Our people at the company weren't parts in a machine, but rather more like members of a community. Everything at work seemed to influence my home life, while it seemed everything at home was influencing who I was at work. The boundaries between my personal and professional life were rapidly dissolving in a good way.

Jim's question—"How do you intend to serve the greater whole?"—helped me to slowly begin to understand at a much deeper level that Vertex's software didn't just calculate taxes for specific corporate customers. It enabled much greater benefits for our corporate customers, their customers, the broader business community, and society at large.

Yet, almost as soon as I recognized this new insight, I also recognized the catch-22 that went along with it. The more I said to others, "See! See how Vertex is connected to everything!" the more they would just look at me as if I had lost my mind. I realized that the only way for others to see the connections that bind us all together was to create an environment at Vertex where they could discover those connections for themselves.

I didn't believe it would be helpful to preach, force, cajole, or require our people to see our place in the world the way I did. Heck, it was enough for people to do their jobs, meet the performance expectations of the company, earn a competitive pay, and go on with their lives. We were building a growing software business, not a cult. After my epiphanies, I had to be careful that I didn't presume to have special wisdom that others at the company would be required to accept.

But what, then, to do? It also didn't seem right to simply pretend that I hadn't made a meaningful discovery or that it wasn't something others could benefit from. How could I help people see what I saw without overstepping my role as a business leader or coercing them into seeing it, or worse, coercing them into pretending they saw what I did?

I knew that my newfound sense of connectedness brought a deep and powerful sense of meaning and fulfillment to my work. No longer did I see myself as having lost my idealistic hope of making a difference in the world. I could now see, with complete clarity, that I was already making a significant difference—I just hadn't realized it before!

Wouldn't others want to not only make an outstanding living but also do so with the awareness that their work was contributing to the betterment of humanity? Who wouldn't want both? As I later became fond of saying, "We can't all join the Peace Corps. Some of us have to make the tax software—but at least it can be *meaningful* tax software!"

The next ten years would prove to be a long and winding road of slow but steady progress toward the dream of meaningful global impact that we created back in 1993. Along the way, my path toward a more meaningful work life was littered with amazing highs and the lowest of lows.

CHAPTER 14

MY INNER COMPASS

When I truly listened to understand Jen, I realized for the first time that my way of viewing the world was just that . . . my way of viewing the world! I was raised to believe that there was a right way and a wrong way to do something, and a right answer and a wrong answer to every question. Recognizing that there could be two right answers to the same question and two right ways of doing something was truly a revelation.

The funny thing was that trying to better understand others led me to discover more about myself. Gradually, I was beginning to understand that I had unwittingly developed a set of beliefs about myself and the world that guided my every feeling and action.

Once I understood how these beliefs were driving my behavior, I realized they were drastically misaligned with the person I wanted and needed to be. The "inner compass" I had developed without even knowing it had four primary components or "poles":

- Seeking approval
- Fearing judgment
- Doing to distraction
- Escaping as denial

As I sustained a practice of observing my behavior and my feelings, I recognized that certain uncomfortable experiences kept repeating themselves, even after I had vowed to change. It was strange to realize that I was being driven by motivations that I didn't even see.

The big aha was recognizing that I was primarily working to gain my father's approval. My father was always stingy with any form of appreciation, and I had never felt that I was good enough in his eyes. While I was somewhat aware of resenting the pressure I felt from him, I was completely blind to my deeper desire to actually earn his appreciation.

Once I began to recognize this, I knew it wasn't healthy for me to aspire to leadership for the purpose of meeting his expectations. That couldn't be the right motivation. Yet I was left wondering what the right motivation should be.

Jim repeatedly asked me, "What do you hope to achieve over the long term?" This prompted me to start looking differently at my long list of to-dos—something I had always been proud of as I checked off item after item.

From the perspective of what I wanted to achieve over the long term, the list made almost no sense whatsoever. These lists were essentially nothing more than a reaction to the latest problems or immediate opportunities. There was no sense of long-term benefit and achievement to them at all. Crossing off items had once made me feel good, but now I was starting to feel a bit lost.

After sharing my concerns with Jim, he introduced me to Stephen Covey's time management matrix* as a way to recognize and address my urgency addiction. The tool categorizes tasks into four quadrants based on urgency and importance:

Quadrant 1: Urgent and Important—Tasks that require immediate

---

* "Manage Your Time and Energy Effectively," *FranklinCovey Blog*, accessed March 13, 2026, https://www.franklincovey.com/blog/manage-your-time-and-energy-effectively.

attention and are critical to your goals like urgent work or personal deadlines, pressing problems, or an unforeseen crisis.

Quadrant 2: Not Urgent but Important—Tasks that are important for long-term success but do not require immediate action like proactive planning, relationship building, and healthy recreational downtime.

Quadrant 3: Urgent but Not Important—Tasks that require immediate attention but do not contribute significantly to your goals like routine paperwork, emails, and reports.

Quadrant 4: Not Urgent and Not Important—Tasks that are neither urgent nor important, often considered distractions like social media scrolling, busy work, and other ways you might procrastinate.

By putting the Covey matrix into practice, Jim helped me see that my "doing" was getting in the way of achieving my more meaningful, long-term goals. I was spending all of my time in Quadrant 3, the Urgent but Not Important issues. The fact was that I thought the urgent was important, and I had no way of actually knowing what was and wasn't important!

After further reflection, I understood that my doing wasn't only getting in the way of achieving my important longer-term goals, but it was also blocking out my constant sense of unease that something wasn't right. I was so busy I had no time to actually think about what I really wanted or why I was working so hard in the first place.

My fond self-image was that I was "Mr. Work Hard, Play Hard," putting in extra hours and extra intensity at work, and then putting in extra hours and intensity in my social life (read: drinking). Heck, it had worked in college where I earned academic honors while also spending a copious amount of time trying to be the life of the party, so no point in becoming old, serious, and boring now, I reassured myself.

But when Jim asked me, "How's your state of being coming into the meeting?" my first thought was *What's a state of being?* My second thought was *What, hungover?* Over time I could see that my partying was a kissing cousin to my addiction to doing.

Whether working or partying, what I was doing was staying so busy and energized that I had no time or energy for even thinking about why any of it mattered. And even less energy for how I might actually be feeling about any of it. My partying was a form of escapism that worked to keep me in denial of the deeper sense that somehow I didn't deserve all the good things that were happening for me.

Of the four poles of my hidden compass, the "fearing judgment" component was perhaps the most striking. I noticed that I would make a decision that I firmly believed was in the best interest of the company but then would apologize to those impacted, as I also believed that they would judge me harshly for my actions. Often, I would find myself apologizing in advance to people before they could judge me!

I was in a vortex of my own making, constantly seeking approval and driving for success while judging myself for possibly hurting people in the process. Fearing judgment became jet fuel for my zeal to do anything I could to create the greatest place to work that ever was, for only then could I calm my anxiety that I didn't deserve any of it in the first place.

At one point, I said to Jim, "I would die for this company." It was my way of saying that the last thing I would ever let myself become was a hard-bitten, callous, self-interested corporate automaton who didn't care about the people he worked with.

REFLECTION

Over the years, I realized that I was ashamed of the position that I had unwittingly assumed. It wasn't fair and I knew it. No matter how well we did, I believed I owed it all to my privileged birth as the oldest son, and not to who I was or what I had contributed.

As it turned out, the revelations of my early thirties, with the help of Jim's steady support and gentle challenge, didn't produce a miracle cure. At first, I thought my newfound self-awareness was like instant karma and would serve to keep me on track. I had no idea that my fragile ego wasn't going to give in without a fight. And fight back it did!

Only after many months and years of self-observation and self-reflection, with Jim's help as well as the help of others, was I able to see the endemic patterns in my behavior and their underlying causes. This growing awareness generally helped me move beyond them.

While these behaviors and feelings do still crop up from time to time, it's never with the same grip as they had on me in my twenties, thirties, and early forties.

And while the motivations based on my hidden compass began to weaken, a new compass began to emerge. This compass had, in the words of Bill George, former CEO of Medtronic, a true north. The more I focused on what I was actively choosing to achieve and who I wanted to be, the more my original patterns slowly gave way to more effective states of being and ways of acting.

As I read more about personal development, it was a relief to learn that everyone has an implicit compass, whether hidden or otherwise. The professional consensus is that all people develop a set of beliefs about themselves and the world, because doing so is essential to becoming an individual capable of acting independently of others. It is essential to becoming one's own person. While your original internal compass may not be all you wish it to be, understanding its poles is essential to understanding why you make the choices you make.

And even if you're not fully aware of these poles, the more you know about them, the more capable you become in finding your true north—advancing toward your ideal work life.

After all, it's your compass that helps you experience meaning, and when it changes, what is meaningful to *you* changes—just as my proud to-do list gradually lost its importance to me.

ACTION STEPS—DISCOVERING YOUR INNER COMPASS

Self-awareness is essential to realize deeper meaning and fulfillment. If you don't know what matters to you and why, it's pretty hard to make more of it. It's kind of like driving up to a gas station and not knowing if your vehicle is powered by diesel, unleaded gasoline, or electricity. What source of energy do you buy?

The catch-22 of self-awareness is that it doesn't come quickly or easily, and it can be a little scary to think, *What if I don't like my internal compass?* The other understandable source of discomfort can come from thinking, *What if I find that I've wasted some of my work life?*

As for the first concern, if you find you don't like something about who you've become, by discovering it you empower yourself to become who you want to be. The upside is way better than being trapped in something you don't understand for fear of understanding it!

As for the second concern, what I found was that every moment of my work life was necessary for me to have become the individual I am today. Nothing was wasted. Without failure and the self-awareness gained through the process, I would be stuck in old paradigms with no way out. The upside of self-knowledge crushes the fear of knowing more about yourself.

Here are a few simple steps that will help you move toward greater self-awareness and develop the ability to create a new internal compass.

1. Find a quiet, reflective space and write out the patterns you observe in yourself. It could be as simple as "I always procrastinate when I have to . . ." or as complex as "I avoid committing to my coworkers, always hedging my bets." List everything you can think of, even if you don't think they are important at the moment.

2. Put away the list you made for a couple weeks. Then return to your quiet, reflective place and ask yourself, "Why do I do

that?" for every pattern of behavior you observe. Make sure to capture your observations.

3. Ask a trusted friend, family member, or colleague to read this chapter and the notes you have taken as a result of your self-observations. Ask this person if they would be willing to be your sounding board on this topic.

4. Get together with your partner in a quiet, reflective place and talk about what you have noticed about yourself and your behavior related to work. You may notice patterns that are work related but also show up at home or socially.

5. Repeat this process every month until you think you have full awareness of your current internal compass.

6. Ask yourself, "What aspects of my internal compass do I want to keep or emphasize, and what aspects do I want to change?"

7. Make a plan and put it into action!

AI NOTE: For this work, AI can be a double-edged sword. It can "get to know you" and provide exceptional education and insight into what your patterns of behavior and feelings may suggest about your beliefs and paradigms, helping you become aware of knowledge and perspectives you may not have been aware of. It can even ask questions to help prompt your self-reflection. What it can't do is muster the courage for you to see yourself and your motivations more clearly. And it can't decide for you why you are the way you are. That's fresh powder for you to ski on. Please consult "how to use AI coaching" tutorials from trusted sources before inviting AI to help you with an experience like this.

CHAPTER 15

IT'S NOT ABOUT THE MONEY

"**A**nd the #1 Best Place to Work in Pennsylvania goes to Vertex, Inc.!"

As our vice president of human resources, Jan Mehnert, and I walked to the front of the ballroom to accept the award, my head was spinning. The company had just been named the Best Place to Work in Pennsylvania, in our first-ever entry into this form of competition.

The large employer category of 250-plus employees included perennially excellent corporate cultures like Vanguard, Harley-Davidson, and Blue Cross of Philadelphia. While we had devoted ourselves for nearly a decade to living our values, I honestly never thought that we would achieve this kind of recognition.

As the event wound down, I was approached by a gentleman I'd met earlier in the evening. He was the executive leader of Harley-Davidson's billion-dollar plant in York, Pennsylvania. Harley had come in twenty-seventh that evening out of hundreds of companies hoping to be recognized. "Congratulations, Jeff! Give me a call. I would like to know what you guys are doing." I am not going to lie; I was blown away that this guy wanted to talk to us!

Fast-forward a month, and there I was at the York plant—along with two of our passionate culture champions, Colleen Kirk and Jim Bailey. We had accepted an invitation from the Harley executive to have lunch with him and some of his key people.

As the luncheon came to a close, the Harley executive thanked us and suggested that I spend some time with the head of organizational development at Harley, Dave Baldwin. "Dave visits periodically, and I will suggest he spend some time with you."

I had no idea why I was accepting these invitations other than it felt good to have someone outside the company who recognized that what we were trying to do was worth their time to understand.

A couple of months later I got a call from Dave Baldwin asking if I was free for dinner that evening in York. Dinner turned into four hours of intense mind melding over the amazing power of true collaboration and what it meant for business systems evolution, performance, and human dignity. We more or less ignored our food, and the time went by in a snap. As we were finally getting ready to part ways, Dave said, "You should meet our CEO, Rich Teerlink. He's in the process of retiring, and he may have an interest in what you are trying to do."

Two weeks later I was cooling my heels in a conference room at the Harley Capital Drive plant in Milwaukee, waiting to meet Rich, and still not really sure why I was there. After maybe ten minutes of staring at the walls, this guy strolls in and says, "Are you Jeff? Hi, I'm Rich. Dave Baldwin says I should listen to what you have to say."

Rich Teerlink, whom I would later realize was a legend at Harley, was asking me to tell him what I thought about people and culture. I was shocked. It was like the same feeling I'd had when the sales team gave me a 3 out of 7 on trust in my first FranklinCovey 360° Assessment—but in reverse.

Not knowing what else to do, I launched into the same speech

I'd given Dave Baldwin. Rich seemed particularly interested in my personal epiphanies and how they'd opened my awareness to the importance of relationships and how powerful it was to listen from the other's point of view.

As the hours passed, Rich listened intently, occasionally asking an open-ended question. I began to realize that he was very different from what I'd expected a public company CEO to be. Like Jim Patton, he seemed genuinely fascinated by what I had to say.

Three hours felt like three minutes. Finally, Rich says, "If you need help with anything, just give me a call," and he handed me his card with his personal cell phone number. I thanked him, though I had no idea at all what I would do with the number of a motorcycle company CEO.

Yet like Jim, Rich seemed to fully grasp what I'd discovered about the meaning of my work life, both personally and professionally. I also got the sense that he knew about all kinds of stuff I didn't yet know.

A few months later, I received a simple email from Rich. All it said was, "It's not about the money." And this from the man who had helped lead Harley out of near bankruptcy, ultimately creating return to shareholders of $30,000 for every $1 invested at the beginning of his tenure.

I would later learn that Rich's secret of success at Harley was in creating a working environment for people that was founded upon the value of mutually beneficial relationships. As he would say to me years later, "Jeff, nothing good happens if people don't trust each other."

Rich became my second mentor, ultimately helping Vertex form a world-class board of directors and create a world-class corporate culture that emphasized the trust we created among our colleagues, customers, partners, and shareholders.

We would go on to be recognized with many Best Place to Work awards. And, during the twenty years of my tenure, our average turnover rate was 4.5 percent in an industry that averaged 17 percent.

Rich passed away in the spring of 2025. He remained my primary mentor until his slide into the grip of dementia made it no longer possible. Even as his memory was failing badly, he would take the time to see me at his home in the Milwaukee suburbs, giving me his undivided attention and asking me, "What's the end you have in mind?"

I was standing in the back of the packed room at his public memorial service, listening to one of his former executives share reflections on his leadership at Harley to the roughly two hundred in attendance, many of whom were former Harley employees. "Rich believed in us more than we believed in ourselves," the former executive shared. Someone in the audience shouted and clapped. Then a few stood, and finally the whole room stood and erupted in applause.

More than a quarter century after his tenure at Harley was complete, Rich Teerlink's colleagues showed me what the real return on investment is for a leader who put the value of relationships before all else. I would never need any more proof that "it's not about the money."

REFLECTION

Rich wasn't alone in his belief about what truly matters at work. Popular books like Alfie Kohn's *Punished by Rewards* and, more recently, Daniel Pink's *Drive* share in-depth findings that most people are not motivated by extrinsic rewards, contrary to the carrot-on-a-stick incentive-based compensation-as-motivation approach many businesses espouse.

Since receiving that email from Rich twenty-five years ago, I've become increasingly convinced of three things:

1. Money does matter. It's essential to meet our fundamental needs.

2. We are motivated by a lot more than money. Once our fundamental financial needs are met, money becomes something we

are glad to have more of, but other, more personal things are ultimately more meaningful.

3. The other things that are more meaningful are different for every person, and they change over time.

For nearly twenty years, I had the privilege of working with a colleague at Vertex named Penny Vennerholm. Penny was exceptional at everything she did and had a remarkable ability to build relationships with people. She lived Rich's wise counsel that trust was built on mutually beneficial relationships. No one who knew Penny would think for a second that she was trying to win at your expense. And she was a national sales leader for Vertex!

What made Penny particularly remarkable was that in spite of the advancing cancer that would ultimately take her life in her mid-fifties, she kept on working. And she didn't have to. She *wanted* to. With her children raised, a husband in a high-paying profession, and having earned a financially rewarding living herself, Penny had no financial need to work. And yet, she kept on doing what she could to be of service to her "Vertex family" as she called us. I would never suggest to anyone that work is more important than family and wellness. What Penny told me was that her work was also a space to live the beliefs of her faith.

To Penny, being there for others so they could grow as people and professionals was the most meaningful thing about her work life. It had nothing to do with the company's financial success or her own compensation. In fact, it never had. In honor of her legacy, Vertex recognizes the individual who did the most to help others succeed with the Shiny Penny award each year.

If the standing ovation at Rich's memorial wasn't proof enough, seeing Penny take calls from her hospital bed, for no other reason but to help others, was incontrovertible evidence that Rich was right.

In the end, at the very end, when all is said and done, it's not about the money.

ACTION STEPS—IF NOT ONLY THE MONEY, THEN WHAT IS WORK ABOUT?

The question isn't, What's more important than money? The question is this: In addition to the money to meet your needs, what is personally most meaningful to you about your work?

Here are six simple steps to help you reflect upon what you find most meaningful about your work:

1. Identify two or three experiences at work where you feel like you made a difference or that you feel personally proud of.

2. What about your work and those experiences matter to you?

3. Ask a friend or colleague to lunch. Share with them your reflections from the preceding steps and invite them to share similar reflections about their work.

4. What new insights or observations can you make about the meaning of your work based on your reflections?

5. Based on your learning, how would you like to approach your work going forward?

AI NOTE: This exercise is almost entirely a self-reflection with the help of a knowledgeable and trusted friend or colleague who knows you, your work, and how you show up in your work life. This is something that AI cannot do. However, you can share your observations and insights with a trusted AI, asking it: "Given what I've learned, what suggestions might I consider to evolve my approach based on the leading experts in the field?"

HOW LONG WILL YOU LIVE?

With a desire to establish a purposeful and collaborative corporate culture anchored in our vision, mission, and values, Vertex created orientation sessions where I would spend time with small groups of new employees. These meetings became an opportunity for me to explore with our newest people the true purpose of the company and what I believed to be the true purpose of all businesses.

It also became an opportunity for new employees to discover a deeper meaning in their work. I did my best not to preach too much, nor did I require any sort of philosophical commitment from anyone. It was purely an introductory conversation intended to lift up the idea that the company existed for a higher purpose than just the bottom line.

With tongue firmly in cheek, I dubbed this orientation session the "fire and brimstone" meeting, precisely because I wanted it to be anything but the classic "Thou shalt do this" dictum from on high that one associates with the term "fire and brimstone." It was just the opposite—I did most of the listening, asking questions, guiding employees along, and sharing my perspective in response to their observations.

I wanted to provide an opportunity for Vertex employees to decide for themselves whether there might be more meaning in their work than just collecting a paycheck.

Each group included eight to fifteen new employees who had joined the company between two and six months prior to the orientation meeting. The incoming employees would range in age and experience from a few years out of college to late career individuals, with most having between five and fifteen years of corporate experience.

All kinds of job functions and skill sets were represented, from senior software architects to entry-level telephone sales and customer service representatives. After gathering together and engaging in some preliminary activities, I would be introduced and would go around the room getting to know each person by name and gaining a sense of their role in the company and their prior experience.

And then the fun began.

Most of the meetings would open with a simple question. "Let's start with something light. Why does business exist?"

Almost every time I asked that opening question, a few intrepid souls, wanting to demonstrate to the CEO that they understood the fundamentals of business, would raise their hands and say something like "To create shareholder value," "To make money," or "To generate profit." Maybe one out of five would offer, "To make quality products that customers want."

At this point, I would ask a question based on a product like clothing or cars that was sure to be part of their personal lives. Picking someone who didn't look too terrified, I would say something like "Those are cool boots you're wearing. Where did you buy them?"

Then we would talk about why they picked that pair of boots, what they liked about them, and how they chose the store, until everyone felt comfortable that I really understood the individual and how they came to buy that specific pair of boots.

That would lead to the question, "Did you buy the boots to help the boot maker make a profit and build shareholder value?"

That was usually met with some chuckles and smiles. The answer was obviously, "Of course not!"—which would then lead to a longer conversation about the real benefit they experienced from the boots, like "They're stylish," or "They keep my feet warm," or "They last a long time."

Throughout, it was obvious to all that as customers we don't feel any obligation to sellers to help them make money. At that point we would pause and consider a question like "Does the retailer exist to help you have a positive experience of their boots or to make money?"

This question would trigger the classic "chicken and egg" conversation, with some members of the group vigorously defending the notion that without money to pay employees, there would be no boots to buy, and others commenting that if the business did not create a return on investment for shareholders, there would be no company to make the boots. Others would retort that without customers to serve, there would be no purpose for the company to exist in the first place. The money and the employees mean nothing if there aren't customers who want boots, they would point out.

After about twenty minutes of back-and-forth, I would then throw a curveball and say to the group, "I will never ask you to come to work and be motivated to make me richer."

This would invariably get people's attention. It's not every day that you meet the CEO and co-owner of a privately held company in a small group, and it's even less likely that he is going to tell you point-blank that he doesn't expect you to be motivated by his financial return.

Employees would often react with confusion. I knew from experience that 99 percent of our people came into the company with two primary assumptions that had never before been examined or questioned.

- **Assumption #1**—You must work to make a living, and there is no more meaning to your work than that (unless you work in government or a nonprofit, where some social purpose is explicit).

- **Assumption #2**—Business exists to make the owners money. Any positive impact beyond that is merely a by-product of the activity of moneymaking.

These assumptions have been accepted for so long that they have become implicit, unconscious beliefs. And now, our new employees were sitting face-to-face with the leader of the company, who was throwing those assumptions out the window and asking them to think, perhaps for the first time, about whether there was something more to not only our company, but all businesses.

At that point, the conversation would turn to what the company did and the impact the company had on the world.

Now, truth be told, corporate tax software isn't often linked to improving the human condition, and surely not a single one of those new employees had joined Vertex to save the world. This is why the meetings always started with clothes, cars, vacations, or other experiences that were personal and directly impactful to the new employee. I found through trial and error that it is much easier to connect to the meaning of a new car than it is to connect to the meaning of the tax software essential to the carmaker who made that car.

The conversation would then probe the depths of what it meant for Vertex to be an essential part of the people's ability to buy new clothes from GAP, vacuum cleaners from Walmart, and just about anything from Amazon. We would talk about the consequences of getting the taxes wrong—from unhappy customers to unhappy auditors, to large fines, and even brand-crushing headlines.

Once we established the meaning of correct tax processing for one client company, we would then talk about the overall impact of getting the correct taxes for ten thousand companies serving literally every person in the country. It would begin to register that without Vertex and our fellow tax solutions providers, business as we know it today literally could not function.

Transactions that happen in the blink of an eye, making it possible to buy anything, anywhere, anytime, and have it delivered to anyone, anywhere, anytime, would not be possible. The whole system would grind to a halt as overworked accountants would have to manually process tax calculations the old-fashioned way, with calculators, pencils, and paper ledger books.

At this point, I'd say about 25 percent of those in attendance would make an immediate and powerful connection, another 25 percent were intrigued but still trying to absorb the message, 25 percent remained politely skeptical, and the remaining 25 percent were just trying to survive their first live interaction with a CEO, completely baffled as to why we were talking about philosophy in a business meeting.

Somewhere near the end of the conversation, as people were letting the ideas sink in and were clearly wondering what, if anything, all of this meant to them, I would often stop and share the following invitation to continue their search for meaning beyond the boundaries of our fire-and-brimstone chat.

"Seems to me that life is in thirds. There is the third where you sleep, the third where you work, and the third where you live. Typically, we think of the third where we are at home in the evenings and weekends as our 'life'; the other two-thirds are just necessary to enable that life, one-third providing money and the final third, rest and recovery. However, it seems to me that if we look a little deeper, we can see that the working third can be just as meaningful and valuable as the living third, enabling us to have two-thirds of our lives that matter more than just the essential money we need, rather than just one-third. That's a 100 percent more meaningful life, and it's there for anyone who wants it."

And then, to underscore the point, I would ask a final question. "How long will you live?"

Confronted with the awkward silence that would naturally follow, I would reflect: "Exactly. None of us knows how long we have on this earth. So, it seems to me that I want every day, every breath to be as meaningful as possible. I don't come to work to make more money; I come to work to make the world a better place. You now have that option, and I leave it to you to decide what you want to do with your life and career.

"If you realize, like a friend and former employee who left the company after this meeting, that what you really want is to carve wooden birds for a living, then by all means, go carve birds. You are highly employable people, and you can work almost anywhere. If you find another line of work more meaningful to you, by all means, go for it!"

After assuring them that we weren't a cult and that they would never be asked if they see greater meaning in their work, I thanked them for their time and attention, and I pledged to never say another word about it to them again.

REFLECTION

Between 1996 and my retirement in 2016, I probably did a hundred of those meetings as the company grew from about one hundred to more than nine hundred people. My purpose in those meetings was simple—to create a compelling invitation for people to decide for themselves why they were there in the first place.

We had created our vision, values, and mission together, with active contributions from all of our people in 1996, and I wanted to keep the sense of freedom to think and decide for oneself as vibrant for people joining the company five and ten years later as it was for those of us who were part of the original experience.

Having been blind to my own motivations for joining the company, only to wake up to them thanks to Jim's encouragement to think about my own purpose, I was trying to invite everyone to consider that perhaps they, too, had deeper motivations of which they might not have been fully aware.

In most conversations it became evident that people were choosing the company or career path because it was the best offer, the benefits were good, or it was a convenient location. After we won the Best Place to Work award, our great corporate culture was frequently referenced, but not once in my thirty-plus years with the company did someone say, "Jeff, I came here to make a difference in the world."

And yet, there we were, making it possible for millions of people to have the things they need, when and where they needed those things, all the while assuring the government that it would get the revenue it needed to ensure that those things got to the stores and homes safely, securely, and efficiently.

Life as we know it couldn't have happened without the technology we were creating at the company, but few if any who joined us had any idea of the larger importance of our work.

My second purpose was to convey to our newest people that I really cared about them as people whose lives and dreams were more important than the work they were doing. What became clear to me through Jim's example was that people aren't "human resources," perhaps the most inhumane term ever created, and that putting the work before the person wasn't just inhumane, it was downright stupid.

People who know they are genuinely cared for will almost always genuinely care for each other and their work. When people feel that their personhood is merely something to overcome in service to getting the work done, well then who can blame them when they adopt an attitude of "not my job" or "what's in it for me?"

Realizing that my own life mattered most as an opportunity to serve others, I wanted everyone to know that they were safe to care for others as well. People would often thank me for the kind of place the company had become, and I always found that odd, since we had clearly created the company *together*, just like we said we would.

ACTION STEPS—WHAT MATTERS ABOUT WHAT YOU DO?

The importance of having a company that cares about you and the relationships you have with your internal and external customers is the topic of another great book, *The Caring Company*, by my longtime friend Dr. Isaac Getz.

Dr. Getz and his coauthor, Laurent Marbacher, tell the stories of many remarkably successful companies that began by caring about the impact they could have and the people they affected before concerning themselves with the money required. This is a recipe for success for many businesses but also holds out hope for any person seeking greater fulfillment from their work life who shares in this belief.

The following steps can help you get in touch with your contributions to your workplace ecosystem of colleagues, customers, and partners. You may experience a shift in perspective from what you are doing to the impact you are having. It's fascinating to see how these dots connect to create something important and even magical and potentially essential to finding the fulfillment you are seeking.

1. Find a peaceful, quiet place to reflect; pause, giving yourself time to quiet your mind.

2. Consider the people you work with and the customers you serve, either directly or indirectly, through the work you contribute to your employer. Capture those contributions.

3. What matters to you about your contribution to these people,
   this work, and these customers?

4. How do the people you work with, the customers you serve,
   and their customers benefit from the products and services
   you help create?

5. Make some notes about what comes up for you and share your
   thoughts with a friend or colleague.

AI NOTE: AI could provide some remarkable additional
perspective around your observations about the benefits you
perceive your colleagues, customers, and their customers
receive from your work. Caution: The value isn't in "getting
the answer" as though you were in school, submitting a
paper. The value is in the search for insight within you. The
paradigm shifts only when you conduct a genuine search for
the meaning of your relationships; only then can totally new
ways of viewing your work and yourself emerge. I recommend
engaging this experience as designed, and after you've come
to your own conclusions, share them with your AI partner for
added perspective.

CHAPTER 17

THE ULTIMATE BOTTOM LINE

Jim Patton and Rich Teerlink were all about supporting my journey toward discovering who I really was and what I truly cared about. They understood that being authentic to myself was more important for becoming an effective leader than anything else.

For example, I had an ex-advertising guy's understanding of finance, which is to say, not much. Rich, who was Harley's CFO before he became CEO, said to me, "Jeff, you know all the finance you need to know. You have a full-time CFO and a former CFO as your audit committee chair on the board. All you need to know is how to learn from them."

Our audit committee chairman, Terry Kyle, joined Vertex's board of directors after helping Shared Medical Systems (SMS) sell to Siemens in 2000. His knowledge of finance was unparalleled, and his skills had been forged in the cauldron of quarterly analyst calls with Wall Street firms and financially motivated institutional investors.

When Rich and Terry first became involved as informal advisors, our board meetings were occasional and the preparation material consisted of a handful of PowerPoint slides summarizing the company's current financial performance, with an emphasis on sharing as little detail as possible.

By the time Terry was through with us, we had seventy pages of board preparation material, with sub-schedules I never even tried to understand. Even though we were private at the time, we acted like a public company with Terry putting us through a rigorous process.

And boy did it pay off. Led by my successor as CEO, David DeStefano, the company had a successful initial public offering in 2020 with a market capitalization of $3 billion.

But there was more to Terry than just being a great numbers guy. He was perhaps the most authentic leader I had ever met.

Terry understood that you had to be who you were and that bullshitting people by trying to be who you weren't wasn't gonna fly with anyone. People may not have liked Terry's style, but they never doubted whether he was telling it like it is. And, like the good coach that he was, he assessed the playing field and quickly determined that Rich was a better fit to do the soft stuff with me, since he could quickly see that we needed a ton of help with the hard stuff that was right up his alley.

Rich and Terry taught me the power of being as real as I could be. And Terry taught me the value of deep expertise. I had always appreciated the expertise of our software engineers and tax specialists. However, it wasn't until Terry sat me down to understand how much I didn't know about accounting and finance that I really came to appreciate how much I never knew about tax or technology either.

But Terry understood what Rich tried to impress upon me. What I needed to do was know enough to respect the many experts in the company. My job was never to know more than those who knew ten times more than I would ever know. My job was to create an environment where diverse experts could do their best work together.

Between board meetings I would visit Terry at his home office above the woodshop in his garage. He called it "The Shed." After catching up, he would ask me what I was concerned about. My mouth would start running on about whatever the issue was until inevitably and authentically, Terry would say something sensitive like "Jeff, when are you gonna shut up so I can talk?"

He would then patiently break down the issue into logical components, address each piece until he thought I understood the gist of it, and then put the pieces together so I could understand the whole picture, or at least the key parts that mattered.

A tutoring session with Terry was often like having a spreadsheet constructed through words and occasionally some numbers written on a yellow pad in pencil.

On more than one occasion, Terry would get excited and delve into the nuances of a particular sub-schedule or gray area of the generally accepted accounting principles (GAAP) only to see the glaze come across my eyes. Then he would say, "You don't care about this, do you?"

To which I would smile and reply, "I truly care that you care, Terr." And to his massive credit, he would accept that I didn't need to know, and he would move on to another point that I actually had to understand.

I honestly don't remember much of the finance that Terry taught me. What I began to see, which was incredibly valuable, was how much I did not understand about every other field relevant to the business. It was humbling, frightening, and liberating.

Humbling because I knew so little. Frightening because I knew I could never know enough to seriously contribute to any of it. And liberating because it helped me feel free to focus instead on the quality of our decision-making and our ability to harmonize diverse experiences into cohesive strategies that benefited from our shared commitment.

My experiences with Terry helped me better understand the analytical mind and also the prevailing perspective of what I considered the old-school corporate world. I came to appreciate that all the inspiration and effective collaboration that I cared about so much wouldn't amount to anything if the software was buggy and the company didn't pay its bills on time and file its own taxes the right way.

What made Terry unique was that in spite of enormous depth in his chosen field, he could shift gears into the realms of philosophy. And when confronted with a new perspective, he would, like Jim and Rich, listen with a completely open mind.

Early in our relationship, Terry shared with me a basic lesson about business: "Jeff, it all comes back to shareholder value. The company exists to return investment to its shareholders. You have to tie everything back to that."

At this time in my life, I was on fire, not only about the larger purpose of the company that Jim had helped me discover but also about the email from Rich saying, "It's not about the money." I looked at Terry, a much larger, stronger, and more, uh, intense guy than I was, thinking, *How am I going to get this across to him?*

I don't know where it came from, but the next thing I knew, I was saying to this hugely successful, deeply experienced former CFO, twelve years my senior, "Would you say that to your customers?"

He looked at me for a few seconds, pondering what had just shot out of my mouth before I could think twice about it. And then he simply nodded, uttering something like "Good point."

And we moved on. After that moment, I knew that his integrity was real and that there wasn't a topic where we would fail to get to a shared understanding so long as we stuck with whatever debate we were having. It was one of the most valuable lessons and one of the most valuable relationships of my career and my life.

REFLECTION

There's a lot of soft stuff in the hard stuff, and there's huge meaning in being an expert in what you know.

In fact, without the experts, all of us soft skills folks would have no people to employ, no culture to nurture, no ads to run, and no sales to make. No expertise? No ambulances, hospitals, food supply, defense systems, movies, or clothes. And experts with no ability to learn from or work well with others will make half the difference of those who can.

The seminal research on meaningful work, conducted by Dr. Marjolein Lips-Wiersma, Lani Morris, and Dr. Sarah Wright and published in several leading academic research publications, clearly affirms that mastery of craft is one of the four major quadrants of meaningful work.*

All work involves some level of expertise. I have personally worked in a book bindery where I lifted pamphlets off a machine for eight hours a day, and I have moved residential furniture, painted houses, and landscaped corporate campuses. I know that all of these jobs required some degree of specialized knowledge. Being an expert and appreciating expertise are deeply meaningful to many people.

Terry taught me that the ultimate bottom line is respect for the deep expertise and experience of others.

ACTION STEPS—EXPERT, KNOW THYSELF

Everyone has some level of expertise, but we often fail to appreciate it in others as well as in ourselves. Remember, expertise in all work is a source of pride and self-worth. It is important for people to feel appreciated for the work they do and the knowledge and effort required.

---

* See the appendix for these publications.

Here are some easy steps designed to increase your appreciation of the value of expertise—your own and that of others.

1. What is it that you do? What were you taught when you first got started? What would you teach a new person who was hired to do what you do? This is your expertise.

2. Do you often reflect on how much you have learned since you began doing this kind of work? Think back to the time before you started this work. Did you have any idea about its specific requirements?

3. Complete this sentence: I have mastered (*this work*) and have developed into an expert at what I do. If I can learn these skills, I can learn other skills and knowledge that I don't currently possess, like (*insert what you might like to learn here*).

4. Do you feel that others appreciate your expertise or even have any idea about what you know? Share your self-assessment with a friend. Then ask them to share their own experience and expertise with you and be sure to appreciate them!

5. Now that you have some experience, repeat this exercise with a different person. Start by asking them to share an appraisal of their own expertise before sharing your own. Thank them for participating in this exercise and for helping you to have a clearer understanding of the work they do and a deeper appreciation for their expertise.

AI NOTE: I asked a leading AI tool, "Who are the top ten experts in the field of meaningful work?" In seconds, the AI returned with an impressive list of experts, most of whom I recognized. The list seemed somewhat biased to me, so I followed up with: "AI, what criteria was used to define 'expert' for the purpose of this request?" The AI shot back that I had indeed asked a good question and that its criteria for "expert" were based largely on academic credentials and publications. So I asked it to redo the search based on "experts with at least fifteen years of actual business experience." It returned a completely different list! The point is this: AI can be an awesome partner, accelerating the growth of your expertise and the appreciation of others. But beware. Under the well-articulated, confident, and brief answer most AI tools will give you in response to a question are many layers of assumptions that it must make in order to give you that answer. And, as any true expert will tell you, the devil is in the details.

CHAPTER 18

WHO'S ON FIRST?

Jim Patton introduced us to the practice of taking ten minutes at the end of every meeting to reflect on the quality of the meeting experience. This was part of a team-building effort and a way to encourage team members to openly share their perspective.

For the first few months, the Vertex leadership team responded as if we were in boot camp. A small (edited for language) sample of some of their comments:

- "A total waste of time."

- "I have no idea what we were trying to achieve."

- "We got nowhere."

- "At least it's over."

I learned quickly that real team building isn't always easy or fun, especially in the beginning.

But I was committed to the belief that together we could achieve more than we could if I simply ran the meetings and drove everyone to a preordained decision without the benefit of their perspective or expertise. As painful as the meetings were, I couldn't see how it would be better if the least experienced person in the room—me—forced everyone into the outcomes I thought best.

My commitment to team building was born in part from our failure with the new software development effort, which was a continual reminder to me of the risk of not working well together. So, I stuck with the approach of creating space for everyone to contribute, actively listening to all, and seeking ways to achieve our shared goals together. Committed or not, it was a real struggle.

A breakthrough came when, after many months, Jim shared with us the concept known as a *task cycle*. This is also called the PPP, which is short for purpose, products, and process.

The task cycle seems simple enough on the surface. Every strategy, project, or even a meeting, would have a **purpose**. That's why the meeting was being held. The purpose would lead to a set of outcomes. These were the tangible results of the meeting, called the **products**, or what you would leave the meeting with. And finally, perhaps most importantly, was the **process**, or the expected flow of the meeting such that it would serve the purpose and achieve the products. The process would replace the typical list of topics that often passes for a meeting agenda.

The PPP could be simply understood as "why, what, and how." Why are we here? What are we trying to achieve while we are here? How do we expect to achieve those outcomes in a way that serves the purpose?

Simple, right? In theory, yes. In practice? Well, that was a different story.

It was remarkable to experience the mess created by a genuine effort by experienced adults as they tried to agree on the first question: "Why are we here?"

As it turned out, the why of any meeting consistently led to the larger question of the why of any strategy, program, or project. And those *whys* led to the question of why the company's goals were what they were and even why the company existed in the first place.

All of a sudden, we went from brutal debates about budgets to brutal debates about why all businesses existed in the first place. In the immortal words of our first software developer and vice president of development, Frank Contigiani, "Are you kidding me?! Do I need a PPP to go to the bathroom!"

As much of a believer as I was, I had to admit that on many occasions it felt as though we were stuck in the middle of that famous Abbott and Costello skit, "Who's on First?" Instead of getting all twisted up about a fictional baseball player named "Who," we were all twisted around a question none of us had seriously considered before, "Why?"

It was clearly a case of growing pains—up until that point, we had all spent our years together doing things without ever being clear about why we were doing them. The *why* was always provided by someone or something else—a parent, a teacher, a boss, or an institution. As we delved into the depths of the *whys* of our work at Vertex, it became painfully evident that none of us saw the same reasons for doing just about anything. It was bizarre, fascinating, and somewhat frightening.

After what seemed like endless iterations, it became clear to all of us that our *whys* consisted of assumptions we had each unconsciously made. As we made them explicit, it became remarkably easier to agree on our *whats* and our *hows*, which included our *whos*. We soon found that when we agreed on why, what, how, and who before committing ourselves to doing something, we rarely (if ever) failed to achieve the outcomes we sought.

Our resilience paid off, and soon we introduced the PPP companywide so as not to deprive our employees of the same growth opportunity we'd experienced. It was a culture-building practice and became a pillar of our new way of doing things.

REFLECTION

Unlike my prior revelations, which happened through seemingly instantaneous flashes of insight, our appreciation of the PPP took years to build. Somewhere in the middle of that struggle we were having lunch with Jim when someone asked, "Jim, could you just tell us how to do this so we can get on with it?" He replied, with a caring smile on his face, "I would. But I don't want to deprive you of the growth."

In hindsight, he was absolutely right. Had Jim simply told us what to do, we wouldn't have believed him or understood. True collaboration couldn't be taught from a book or in a classroom. It had to be forged from experience.

It's like swimming. You could read a hundred books on the topic, watch movies, or attend lectures and you would have no idea what it feels like or how to actually do it. It has to be experienced to be understood, and it has to be practiced to be perfected.

The same is true of collaboration, truly working together with others toward shared ends. The secret is to first seek to understand yourself and then seek to understand others. Then, and only then, should you ask questions with a truly open mind about why, what, how, and who.

Like learning any skill, sport, or musical instrument, collaboration is awkward, painful, and confusing at first. You may often feel like you will never be able to hit the ball, strike the chord, or make the pass. But after hundreds or thousands of repetitions, you start to feel a sense of mastery that will never leave you. Today, at sixty-four, I can walk on to any basketball court and make five of ten foul shots, even if I haven't touched a basketball in five years.

Learning the why, what, and how of what you do with others at work is like that, born of practice.

ACTION STEPS—GETTING TO KNOW YOUR WHY

This book isn't about team building or transforming organizations into collaborative enterprises. It is about helping individuals develop work lives with deeper meaning and fulfillment. I share the preceding story because it is the path I followed that led me to understand what the process involved.

Most of us aren't in a situation where we are part of a group that shares a common commitment to shared leadership, and few if any have a Jim Patton to provide continuous support. However, you can learn more about yourself, and the why, what, and how of your work life, on your own and with the help of a caring friend or colleague.

The who in this case is you! Let's consider your *why*, *what*, and *how*.

1. Refer back to chapter 12 and "The Five Whys" to refresh yourself on what matters most to you about the work you do and the impact that work has on your life.

2. Now reconsider the following question: If you were to serve your *why* in the best way possible, what would your work life look and feel like ten years from now? Why ten years or more? So you look beyond the scope of your current ability, resources, and assumptions. Represent this image of your desired future in the form of words or sketches. It might help to ponder this question while taking a walk in the woods or sitting on a beach.

3. You now have your *why* and a description and picture of your future *what*. Looking back from that future, ask yourself, "How did I get here?"

4. Ask a caring, open-minded friend or colleague to meet with you. Share your *why*, *what*, and *how* with them. Ask them

just to listen and ask questions rather than giving you help or feedback. As you share, notice your feelings and any insights that come to you. Make notes and, based on your feelings and insights, refine your personal PPP (purpose, products, process—in other words, why, what, and how).

5. From your new long-term perspective, make a plan of what you'll need to do this year to begin to move along the path that will bring you to your vision of your ideal work life. Be prepared! Your aspiration will attract opportunities and challenges that you'll need to achieve your goals. Remember, everything, absolutely everything, presents something you can use to realize your dream.

AI NOTE: If you have been reading these AI notes, you should be able to anticipate this guidance: Only you can create your *why* and *what*. Your dream *why* and *what* are equal parts head and heart, so they must be given life by you. AI can be a big help on your *how*, proposing possibilities, scenarios, and helping you assess real-world risks and opportunities.

CHAPTER 19

BABY, WE WERE BORN TO LEARN

The sequence of epiphanies triggered by Jim Patton's gentle but continuous challenge to clarify the purpose, vision, and desired outcomes we sought in our work led me to a simple conclusion—I had a monstrous *why* blind spot. And apparently so did just about everyone else I knew.

And then I heard a psychologist talk about how children learn, and my world was rocked once again. His point was shockingly simple. Children are born learners. They learn to walk and to talk by watching others. They are naturally driven to learn and grow. The desire to learn and grow is born into them. They don't need to be motivated to learn to walk and talk; they are naturally motivated to understand and participate in the world around them.

I don't know if my jaw actually dropped when I heard his words. But I remember exactly where I was standing—in a field below where we live, out walking on a beautiful day—when I realized that what children do naturally is precisely 180 degrees opposite from the way I was taught in school.

My next thought was, *Oh no, if we go the traditional route, we're going to train our own kids for a world that probably won't exist when they are my age. They need to think for themselves and create new meaning with others, and all the stuff they need to know will be at their fingertips.*

Jen took the lead, and the kids weren't put in school. We joined the board of a community of families who believed that children learn naturally and don't need the structure and hierarchy of a traditional school system.

Our three children all participated part-time at the community's resource center (a farm-like campus, more like a home than a school, pursuing experiences of interest to them and their peers). Jen was the general manager of their learning experience. In response to what she knew they needed and what they were interested in, she coordinated their time at the community campus as well as with a variety of tutors and a bevy of parents and other educators in music, art, design, cooking, fashion, and media production in addition to the academic staples of math, English, history, and so on.

Given the freedom from fixed school attendance requirements, we were able to travel at off-peak times to share the wonders of the country and world with our children.

The lessons we were learning at home about how our children learned best on their own terms and were motivated by their own interests transferred well to the workplace. There, those lessons helped me stay largely hands-off from the work of building and selling world-class tax software. Just as I observed our kids learning through trial and error, I understood that business is a similar process of learning by trial and error, or what we tend to call "experience."

I also noted that our kids didn't learn in a linear sequence, nor did they learn the same way or demonstrate the same strengths. Each child was clearly brilliant in their own way. Two of our children were gifted speakers and were both also accomplished stage performers. Our middle son was more reserved; he formed his thoughts carefully and was less likely to express himself in a barrage of words. And yet, when he talked, the veracity of his insight was clearly as advanced as the other children.

The same could be said about my colleagues at work. While a few of us were likely to carry most of the dialogue in any collaboration, putting words to thoughts, others were more likely to reserve comment until they had formed a serious insight or conclusion. When they spoke, we listened closely.

A consultant said to us one day, "Extroverts talk, then think, then talk. Introverts think, then talk, then think." It struck me that this was a truth that I had never before appreciated. Up to that point, I had firmly believed—being extroverted to the extreme—that extroverts were just smarter than those who didn't move as fast as we did.

It was humbling to witness the truth unfolding before me at work and at home. What I was witnessing was unmistakable. The introverts were not only as smart and as fast as the extroverts, but they were far more likely to think with greater depth. It was increasingly evident that while style had value, it was not to be confused with substance.

This was an important lesson, learned at home, with massive implications for transaction tax software engineering. No matter how good we felt or how pretty the package, that software had to perform with accuracy and reliability or we wouldn't last another year in business.

Sales and marketing mattered if we were going to build relationships and grow, but if we didn't have the expertise, rigor, and discipline to engineer solutions that worked better than any other firm, we would soon close up shop, unable to make any positive contribution to the world, much less to our customers, employees, and shareholders.

What I learned at work was that the lessons engrained in us during our school years—that there was a single right answer and that the teacher knew best—were pretty much hurdles to overcome in the workplace. There, the leader usually did not know best, and the best answers changed from week to week and month to month as the facts and circumstances constantly evolved.

By freeing our children to learn based on their own intrinsic curiosity and doing my best to create an environment where the same was true at work, I believed we would realize a more agile, creative, cohesive, and continuously evolving and innovating approach, one destined to win in the marketplace and in the journey of life.

All three of our children graduated college with strong marks. As young adults, each is pursuing their passion in careers that give them deep personal meaning and fulfillment. Our daughter has published two fantasy novels, one son is launching a fashion brand, and our youngest son, having established a career in film production, is creating a new career in design engineering.

As Bruce Springsteen once (sort of) sang, "Baby, We Were Born to Learn."

REFLECTION

Whether in a structured work environment or traditional schooling environment, the essential element is to connect the activity to something real that matters to the learner.

Developing sales tax software that makes it possible for scientists to cure cancer became my *why* at work. For others, it might be making it possible for satellites to connect people in small villages to the global economy.

As I have traveled around the world, talking with hundreds of adults in all kinds of careers and young people in all kinds of learning environments, what I have found is that when given the opportunity to consider the meaning of their learning and work, they often connect to something that is truly personal and important to them.

And even if they can't find that connection, if they consider what might be meaningful to others or what kind of learning or work could be meaningful to them, they can create a spark for the future.

ACTION STEPS—MAKE LEARNING MORE MEANINGFUL

The following simple steps, when repeated over time, can lead to a much deeper connection between what you do and who you are at school, in any learning activity, and at work, whatever that work might be.

1. What are you learning or creating at school, in education, or at work?

2. Why is that learning and work being undertaken? What purpose does it serve?

3. Is that purpose important to you? If so, why? If not, why?

4. What is meaningful to you about the material and skills you are learning or the work you are doing? Are you developing new abilities? Meeting new people? Discovering new insights? Realizing what you want or don't want? Having an impact on someone else?

5. Ask a friend or colleague to join you for a walk or lunch and share your observations. Ask them about the meaning of their learning or work. Does your conversation suggest any new insights for you?

AI NOTE: This is a self-reflective experience with limited potential for additional value from AI. The risk with AI's incredible ability to do work for you is that it does work *for* you. Think about it this way: If you want to become a competitive runner, would you ask AI to go running to get you in shape? You can't get in work life shape by asking AI to do all of the exercising for you. This one's on you.

CHAPTER 20

UGLY WRAPPING PAPER—PART 2

The second half of the 1990s had been very good for Vertex. The advantage we developed by creating the only complete solution to the sales tax calculation and filing process enhanced our reputation as the market leader. Fueled by corporate investment in business systems triggered by Y2K (the feared year 2000 software bug) concerns, our sales grew dramatically.

The millennium came and went, and thankfully the world didn't come crashing to its knees. Software systems had been updated, and business operations the world over did not miss a beat. What did come crashing down, however, was demand for new business software systems.

The 35 percent year-over-year growth that the company enjoyed from 1996 to 2000 slowed to single digits. And not soon after Y2K, the planes came crashing into the Twin Towers, causing the global economy to crash with it.

While we were careful to avoid hiring too aggressively as revenue exploded, our expense growth rate was now higher than our much-reduced growth in revenue, and that meant profit margins were getting seriously squeezed. Unlike many companies in the business software sector, our revenue continued growing due to ongoing tax updates and maintenance services, but there was a clear downward trend in profits.

It was against this backdrop that our two new independent board members, Rich Teerlink and Terry Kyle, asked me to go to lunch. I thought it was going to be another meaningful exchange about strategy or the development of the company culture, and I arrived in high spirits as usual.

We got seated and shared the usual pleasantries. My memory is somewhat fuzzy, but the subsequent conversation went something like this:

Rich: Jeff, how are you feeling about cash flow?

Jeff: We're OK, and once sales pick back up, we'll be fine.

Terry: What if sales don't pick back up?

Jeff: [Silence.]

Terry: How long do you think you have before the company starts losing money?

Jeff: I'm not sure. Maybe three months. But we can't cut expenses; we have to stick with the investment in the next-generation solution.

Terry: Of course you do. But if you start losing money, you'll be digging a hole that will be hard to climb out of. And you can't raise prices.

Jeff: Sales will bounce back soon.

Terry: And if they don't, what then?

Jeff: [Silence.]

Rich: Jeff, it has to be done, or you'll run out of cash.

Jeff: [More silence.]

They were being as supportive as they could be while making it clear that the only way to survive the aftermath of the dramatic slowdown in sales post Y2K was to significantly reduce our expenses. And the only way to do that was to let people go.

I was crushed. I had been desperately holding on to the hope that sales would bounce back to their pre-Y2K growth levels; I didn't want to accept that we couldn't defy gravity. More than that, I genuinely loved our people and couldn't imagine being responsible for the pain that they would suffer.

I had convinced myself that we were, and that I was, special and that the rules of business that applied to everyone else would magically never apply to us. My cherished self-image was that I had been granted a special insight and that it would effectively shield me, and all of us, from adversity.

As the truth of their wisdom settled in, I excused myself and went to the men's room. Returning a few minutes later with eyes bloodshot and wet, I told them I understood. Eventually, we let go of 7 percent of the workforce, including people I had known since high school and who I considered to be part of my extended family.

Rather than strategize the staffing changes in secret and then create an event out of drastic changes all at once, we announced that we would need to reduce expenses. We asked people to discuss the changes among themselves, make suggestions for improvements, and otherwise attempt to make intelligent, respectful decisions.

It was extremely difficult for everyone involved. I personally struggled with whether I should lay myself off, I was so distraught over feeling as though I had failed everyone. If I were to lead by example, I thought I should go first.

Jim and others helped me understand that business cycles happen and we had done better than most. "How could you help anyone from the sidelines?" Jim asked. And so I stayed, a decision that never felt entirely right but seemed satisfactory over time.

Ultimately, the company grew stronger from the experience. Blind spots in our planning processes were lifted up, and those processes were improved. Our people rallied together, supporting each other through the uncertainties and ambiguity.

Through it all, we did sustain our investment in the next-generation solution that was under development at the time. It was a platform that has remained the leader in global transaction tax processing twenty-five years later. The boom we experienced between 1996 and 2000 not only cemented our market leadership position, but it also completed our clients' transition from mainframe systems and home-grown software to enterprise resource planning software provided by the behemoths of our industry, SAP and Oracle.

It was a position we would steadily build upon as trust in our relationships with our colleagues, partners, and clients grew and matured, and our business expanded around the world as clients sought a single provider to meet their global requirements.

REFLECTION

Years later I was able to look back and realize that yet again, adversity had proven to be a gift in ugly wrapping paper. As sales plummeted in the early months of the year 2000, and as it became apparent later that year that what had happened wouldn't quickly correct itself in a matter of months, we became numb. The business had been growing like crazy, and we had felt as though anything we did would turn out well.

Still smarting from the embarrassment of the new product's withdrawal in 1992, we had made massive efforts to improve the quality of our processes, our products, and our sales and support capabilities. For the first time, we were a firm that knew what it took to succeed and how to exceed our clients' expectations. However, this maturation had given us a misguided sense of control, even inevitability.

The post-Y2K revenue decline was a massive shock to our system. We hadn't understood that it wasn't our company that was creating demand, it was the macro environment within which we'd operated. When the CEOs and CFOs at our client companies decided that "we're not buying software," it didn't matter what the people in the tax departments said about how our software could save money and reduce their risk. Software was not to be purchased.

It was clear: The macro environment was the dog, and we were lucky to have been the tail. The lesson for me personally was that no matter what kind of success I might be having at any point in my life, I am not in control, and things can change, sometimes for obvious reasons and at other times in completely unpredictable ways.

And yet, with every bout of adversity there was a lesson to be learned and growth to be had. That insight would come in handy in the years to come.

ACTION STEPS—EMBRACING ADVERSITY

Few of us will go through a career without encountering some form of adversity—developments beyond our control that change the trajectory of our careers. Those developments may be in our businesses, like having one's company bought by another, losing our funding, or finding that we're not able to fend off a new competitor or disruptive innovation.

Those developments can also happen at home in the form of changes that impact our work lives either directly or indirectly. A child may have special needs that demand attention that can only be provided in another city. Our spouse may attract a new opportunity that is ideal for their career but requires changes in our own. Or some event may put strain on the family's finances, demanding changes that can't be met in the current working and living arrangements.

It is a well-known truth that the attitude of the individual is highly predictive of the outcome they will realize as they navigate work life adversity. Those who see change as opportunity are far more likely to discover opportunity than those who see change as an unfair crisis.

All change is meaningful! The question is what meaning we choose to make of it.

Here are a few simple questions to help you navigate change in a way that is meaningful to you and help you gain greater fulfillment from the experience.

1. What changed? Why did it change? What role did you play in the change that happened?

2. How do you feel about the change? Focus on identifying feelings like excited, scared, or anxious rather than focusing on theories about what happened and why.

3. Get together with a friend or colleague and share your feelings. Then, with your friend as a sounding board, brainstorm together the possible opportunities presented by the change. What does the change make possible, or require, that could lead to positive outcomes?

4. Reflecting on your ten-year dream work life, how can this change move you further toward your goal? Be creative and think the unthinkable!

5. Being pragmatic, what are your options to meet your immediate needs while you further develop the insights that came to you in responding to questions 1–4? This is your plan.

AI NOTE: In this situation, your context has changed materially. AI can be of enormous help to speed and improve your understanding of what the change of context may mean. It can help you assess risks and opportunities. It can help you imagine potential scenarios that may or may not unfold, but by considering them, you can become more agile and adaptable in the face of the unknowable future. Remember, AI can't predict the future!

CHAPTER 21

I'M FINE, NO REALLY!

While the company was navigating the Y2K yo-yo of massive growth followed by a slump in demand, my family of origin was navigating a much more important development. My mother, who had been diagnosed with breast cancer back in 1994, had a recurrence of the disease in 1999.

Antoinette "Nettie" Passo was the oldest of five children born to Sam and Angelina Passo. Both of her parents came from immigrant families from the Calabrian region of Italy.

My mother's Drexel University senior yearbook listing describes an achiever's achiever. In addition to being captain of both the field hockey and lacrosse teams, she ended up leading just about everything else she got involved in. It was, therefore, no surprise that after helping my father get Vertex off the ground while raising three children, she created a "Best of Philadelphia" day spa and later cofounded BreastCancer.org with Dr. Marisa Weiss.

Outwardly, my mother wouldn't have impressed anyone as a feminist, but she was hell-bent on breaking through the barriers women had faced in society and business for generations. She was also deeply committed to raising a son who was more in tune with the needs of women than most men of her generation.

In the 1960s and '70s—the years of my upbringing—gendered roles and attitudes in the home were still remarkably old world. I was only one generation removed from the traditions of old Europe, so I was raised in the midst of transition with my father upholding the old standards and my mother carefully embracing the new ideals.

This created a bit of a catch-22 for me. The message I constantly received from my father was that I needed to be more of his concept of what a man should be—tougher, stronger, and less vulnerable. "If you don't stop, I'll give you something to really cry about" was a common refrain when I was young.

My mother's message was to appreciate her, my sisters, and the roles that women played. I was expected to do the "man's work" in the yard and garage and also participate in doing some of the dishes, vacuuming, and laundry, historically "women's work."

Growing up, before I entered the working world, I sought to emulate my mother's example because I found my father's iron fist to be frightening, and while I would comply, I would never give the full effort I was capable of. As I matured into young adulthood, I believed myself to have become a modern person, very much attuned to the history of oppressive treatment toward women and all people different than I was.

As I entered the family business, I found myself terribly torn between the sensitivity my mother wanted me to have and the desire to demonstrate to my father that I could lead effectively and generate results. This often led to me making decisions that were anything but "sensitive."

This seesaw battle within myself continued as my mother's health rapidly declined. As I turned forty, I found myself unable to confront my feelings. At one level, I had an all-abiding confidence in the spiritual truth of life and death. I believed that all things happen in service to our collective advancement and that no life and no death is meaningless.

My mother passed away from breast cancer in November of 2004. Sustained by my spiritual convictions, I genuinely thought I was fine. At the same time, I ended my seven years of self-imposed abstinence from drinking. I resumed my partying ways just about exactly as I had left off.

It never dawned on me at the time that my drinking and my mother's decline could have been related. Believing that all things, even the most painful, were secretly gifts in disguise, I chugged along, deceiving myself into believing that I was fine and the universe would provide.

REFLECTION

With the gift of hindsight and some help, I can now easily see that while my spiritual understanding was a tremendous source of comfort, I was completely unable to recognize the grief I was experiencing. My inability to accept and actually feel my grief left me in a depression I wasn't able to recognize.

The only way I knew to try and calm a deep discomfort that I couldn't understand was to numb and distract myself with alcohol. Convincing myself that I had learned to control my drinking, I picked up right where I had left off seven years before.

My parents raised me in a way that taught me there were only two acceptable emotions, happy or angry, and only my father was really allowed to be angry. Terrified of his anger, I learned early on to repress my own anger, to the point where I genuinely believed that "I don't get angry." My mother's passing demonstrated that not only did I repress anger, but I did the same with all unhappy emotions, including grief, perhaps the unhappiest emotion of them all.

But of course, I did get angry, sad, scared, and hurt, even if I didn't recognize these feelings or allow them to surface at the time. Driven to demonstrate that I could succeed in business, anxious to be sensitive to others as my mother had wisely encouraged me to be, angry and sad but unable to recognize these feelings, I wound up becoming a rather twisted knot of mixed but unrealized emotions, all the while pretending, especially to myself, that "I'm fine."

And what the heck—I had quit drinking once on my own for seven straight years! If I needed to, I could quit again. I mean, what could go wrong?

I was fine, really.

ACTION STEPS—HOW ARE YOU FEELING, REALLY?

Feelings are fundamentally human and are one of the major human attributes that set us apart from machines, including AI. While AI can act like it has feelings, in reality all it is doing is mirroring words that a person with feelings might say. It cannot actually feel.

People actually feel feelings! A warm sensation when experiencing a beautiful sunset. A sense of calm and safety when embraced by a loved one. A pit in the stomach when one realizes they have made a costly mistake. Sobbing uncontrollably at the loss of a friend or loved one.

We are human. We feel. And it's perfectly OK.

What turns out to be pretty risky is denying our feelings or growing insensitive to them. It also tends to be pretty risky to simply give in to our feelings without thinking and to act impulsively, only to find out that a deep breath and some calm thought might have saved us even greater heartache.

When it comes to creating a more meaningful and fulfilling work life, a huge key is to learn to recognize, experience, understand, and honor our feelings, including the beliefs we hold that influence them and remembering that we don't stop being human and feeling when we're at work.

Here are five simple steps to help you recognize, honor, and embrace your natural ability to feel, especially in work situations.

1. Describe a work situation that elicited feelings other than "fine." What happened? How did you feel about what happened?

2. Describe another work situation that elicited different feelings from those in step 1. What happened, and what did you feel in that situation?

3. Try to identify work situations where you experienced the following feelings—joy, resentment, curiosity, fear, satisfaction, anger.

4. Consider the situations you've identified thus far. Reflect on your experiences and the feelings that you had during these experiences. Do you see any patterns?

5. On a scale of 1 to 5, where 1 is "completely," and 5 is "not at all," rate yourself on your comfort with feeling your feelings, your ability to accept them, and how well you choose actions that honor your feelings. Now think about how to integrate your feelings and your thinking into the choices you make at work.

AI NOTE: This one is all on you. The last step might benefit from some AI-generated input, but here's the thing. Motivation can only come from within you. At best, suggestions from family, friends, mentors, colleagues, or AI are someone or something else's view of what you could or should do. If you are going to act with confidence and commitment—two essential ingredients for success in anything—you need to be certain that any change you make is coming from a deep place of personal conviction, not doing what others, including AI, think you should.

CHAPTER 22

DANGER! SUCCESS STRAIGHT AHEAD

Thanks to the perseverance of our employees, who by now numbered over two hundred people, we managed to give birth to a new flagship offering in 2004. By 2005, the market had rebounded, and our new platform, designed to meet the expectations of the internet era, put us back on a strong growth trajectory.

At that point in my career, I thought the painful experiences of the Y2K retrenchment, the ensuing layoff, and the loss of my mother would serve to permanently deflate my ego. But that didn't turn out to be the case.

Unable to confront my grief, I devoted myself to our collaborative culture, applying the tools Jim Patton had given us with increasing success. At the same time, I resumed the same work hard/play hard attitude that I thought had served me well in my twenties and early thirties.

With numerous Best Place to Work awards, a strong market leadership position, substantial business growth, a vibrant culture, and a beautiful family with our children entering their teenage years,

I thought I had it all. But my ego got the best of me, and with it came a return of the nagging sense that what we had achieved wasn't good enough.

The reality was everything wasn't perfect.

While the core business was thriving, the strategic acquisition we made as we emerged from Y2K was struggling mightily to realize my vision for it, placing an increasing drag on the entire business. The leadership approach that seemed to work so well at our headquarters in Berwyn, Pennsylvania, wasn't working at all well at the Sarasota, Florida, offices of the acquired firm.

The premise of the acquisition was to parlay the new capabilities and market position into a new, all-inclusive offering. This would have been a fourth major transformation of the company and was our first time integrating new people, new technology, and an outside culture.

The success of the core business masked the depth of the challenges with the new strategy. I was not only in denial about my grief at the loss of my mother, but I was also deep into the delusion that my dream of the all-in-one corporate tax solution would magically succeed if we just stuck with it.

And stick with it we did, for more than ten years, in the increasingly vain hope of a breakthrough. All that time the core business kept growing and growing and growing—masking the failure of the acquisition.

With the growth and evolution of our customers' needs, we were also confronted with three additional strategic demands. We had to provide a fully global solution, a down-market solution to protect our flank from competition moving upmarket toward us, and a solution for the emerging cloud technology era.

The market was doing what markets do, constantly changing and evolving. With three new strategies, significant core growth, new remote operations, global partnerships to cultivate, and offices to open, it was a blur of activity. Luckily the top and bottom lines looked great.

But the lines on my face were starting to show the wear and tear. I relied heavily on our remarkable team to do all the real work, relegating myself mostly to managing the board and advocating for our strategy. By 2010, the company had grown to approximately five hundred employees, including a half dozen in our new London office with plans drawn up for an office in Brazil as well.

Everything was going great. So why did I feel so awful?

REFLECTION

Our company culture was exceptional on many levels. It was important to me to demonstrate my respect for the organization that we had nurtured into being—we had so many talented and committed people who had so much expertise.

As I saw it, my job was to create a space where people could work well together and pursue what Rich called "mutually beneficial relationships" inside the company and with our partners and clients.

Our approach was clearly working well overall, but it left me feeling isolated. Isolation is inherent in the role of a CEO. It seemed as if all I was doing was attending to others' needs, with everyone wanting or needing something from me that I didn't feel I was able to give.

The better we did, the more I felt the need to numb the nagging feeling that I wasn't truly deserving of any of it. At the same time, I felt that there had to be more. From my current vantage point, I now see that this was a false reality of my own making.

I had unknowingly fallen back into the trap of driving full speed with the brakes on, having success and feeling like a failure. I was feeling both special and worthless at the same time. Only one strategy seemed to cool the constantly overheating engine—alcohol. As much of it as I could get while keeping the car on the road.

ACTION STEPS—DEALING WITH EMOTIONAL OVERLOAD

Whether as a result of unexpected success or failure, we can all enter periods in our work lives that can be best understood as emotional overload. I define emotional overload as a point where the intensity and complexity of our emotions is greater than our ability to understand, accept, and navigate them in a healthy way.

Having been raised in an environment where we didn't really talk about feelings and where one parent was free to be angry while everyone else was expected to be happy, I had limited tools with which to deal with my own emotional overload. Those limits included the inability to even sense what I was actually feeling.

Denial of grief, complex success, and typical midlife challenges at home combined to create an obsessive need to stay busy, seek escape, and self-medicate. While I sought some outside help during this time, my rigidly protected self-image and the depth of my pain prevented me from truly accepting the full scope of my inner conflict.

This was my situation, which may not apply to you at all. You may be completely adept at managing your emotions and never experience any form of overload. But if you're facing your own emotional challenges or feeling a sense of overload, here are some steps designed to help you check in with yourself emotionally.

1. Describe your current state of emotional well-being. Consider major work and life events over the past five years. Consider your significant relationships. Do you sense any areas where you may be feeling fear, uncertainty, grief, stress, anxiety, resentment, confusion, or other difficult-to-navigate feelings?

2. Seek out a friend, caring colleague, mental health professional, or Employee Assistance Program resource. Share with them what you identified in step 1. You don't need to solve anything. Just share how you are feeling.

3. Consider the value of belonging to a group in some shared activity both inside and outside of work. It could be as simple as a group that has lunch together once a month, or a volleyball or gardening group. Belonging is a powerful antidote to feelings of isolation and emotional overwhelm.

4. Mark your calendar to make a date with your friend every quarter to meet privately and update them on how you are feeling about all aspects of your work life. Offer to be a caring listener for your friend should they want to share about their feelings. Again, there is no need to solve anything. Just listen to each other and try to accept that sometimes life is just plain hard and often unfair.

5. At the end of the year, look back over the four meetings and the group activities, and ask yourself, "How am I doing with acknowledging and accepting my feelings?"

AI NOTE: As with anything regarding your feelings and beliefs, AI can be a useful mirror, but it cannot replace the work you must do to see and act on the reflection. Many accomplished psychologists are working hard to develop AI coaches that can make coaching available to anyone at a fraction of the cost of a human coach, guide, or mentor. The early findings suggest that AI bots can provide a valuable experience. However, risks have surfaced that cause me to suggest that you take care in choosing an AI coach.

(**Author's Note:** The preceding steps are intended to be generally beneficial for most people in typical work and life circumstances. These steps do *not* constitute professional advice. Should you recognize any patterns of self-medication, self-harm, harm of others, or suicidal thoughts, seek the assistance of a qualified professional immediately. See the appendix for potential resources.)

CHAPTER 23

HITTING THE WALL

As my fiftieth birthday loomed ever closer, it was increasingly evident that a chasm was growing between how I appeared on the outside and how I felt on the inside. I had accomplished so much, but it wasn't enough to overcome the sense of guilt I felt at having been given such an exceptional opportunity in the first place.

I held on to the belief that the company would have to demonstrate another major leap forward. I thought we needed to prove that a people-first culture could create not only great, but explosive business results. While our culture was working well, the all-in-one strategy I championed to make that leap wasn't following suit.

Rather than accept this increasingly evident truth, I held on to a self-defeating, isolating narrative that only I had the depth of vision and the long-term perspective to fully see the wisdom of the strategy. I truly believed that with persistence, it would prevail. What I didn't realize was that, like the emperor with no clothes, everyone but me could see the truth. And I didn't realize that I had adopted more of my father's reticence to share my inner thoughts than I had ever believed.

The only way I knew to try and calm my growing unease was to distract myself with partying, something for which I had a bottomless appetite. My denial of the underlying malaise in the business was matched by my denial of the underlying, and worsening, malaise in my relationship with alcohol.

What had been an occasional bender turned into a series of increasingly ugly incidents. I couldn't see that my former ability to keep it all together was falling apart. On June 26, 2011, the work hard/play hard ethos I had been so proud of ran into a brick wall. In front of my family and friends I got into an ugly physical altercation with an old friend.

That experience turned out to be the jolt I needed to see that my life was spinning out of control. A month later I checked into an alcohol rehabilitation facility for treatment.

REFLECTION

Having had a seven-year stretch in my thirties where I didn't drink, I was pretty confident that I could learn how to stop drinking permanently. It didn't occur to me until I was in rehab for a few weeks that I was actually an alcoholic. This wasn't a character flaw as I first thought, but a disease, and things would only get worse, not better, if I didn't accept my reality.

This recognition was another revelation. Looking back now, with fifteen years of continuous sobriety, I actually feel grateful for my alcoholism. Without it, I could not have experienced the life I have today, and I would not have developed the ability I now have to be of even greater service to the people who have given me so much.

The long-held idea that my father was the problem and the nagging sense of not being good enough have given way to forgiveness and acceptance. I realize that my dad was doing the best he could and that our relationship was meaningful and necessary for me to become the person I am today. I learned to forgive and accept in order to move forward.

Holding myself in a state of shame or regret over past mistakes will not enable me to be happy today, nor will it help me be of service to those who I may have hurt or negatively impacted along the way.

I no longer feel this intense need to gain others' approval, to self-destruct, or to save the whole world. It's enough to be of service to the greater good in the best way that I can. And I have a whole new cadre of friends who accept me as a true peer; we all work to remain free from our disease for just one more day.

With the hindsight of fifteen years of sobriety, I can say that my alcoholism is yet another gift in ugly wrapping paper. The work I have done to sustain and grow my sobriety has given my life, and my work, deeper meaning, and I feel a depth of fulfillment beyond my wildest dreams.

ACTION STEPS—WHAT TO DO AFTER HITTING THE WALL

I hope you don't hit a wall in the same spectacular and shocking way that I did. It isn't necessary to get to the next level of your journey toward an ideal work life. However, a work life spent avoiding risk or embarrassment may not ever get you to where you truly want to go.

There's truth in the old saying we grew up with: Nothing ventured, nothing gained. Remember, too, that hitting a wall can be a very different experience for each person.

For one person, simply having their work criticized can feel like a calamity. For another, it could be an inappropriate relationship at work or an embarrassing comment. Someone else might be certain that AI will make their skills redundant; someone else has their job eliminated outright.

If you do hit a wall in your work life, here are some simple steps you can take to gain as much growth as you can from the experience.

1. What happened, is happening, or do you fear is going to happen? What is your wall? What makes it a wall for you? What are the consequences that give you concern or fear?

2. Reach out to a caring friend, colleague, family member, or professional. Share with them what is happening or what you fear may happen and be honest about your feelings.

3. Together with your friend, seek out relevant expert assistance. There are many free and confidential resources available to people facing many different kinds of personal and professional challenges. See the appendix for a list of those resources.

4. Sustain your effort. Most of these issues do not get resolved overnight. The experience may be traumatic, creating some lasting impact on your ability to work effectively. Check in with your friend at least every three months to discover whether you are OK and still doing what you need to do to care for yourself.

AI NOTE: The genuine care of a true friend, family member, colleague, clergy, or counselor is the proven source of support and encouragement for people navigating a serious work life situation. I am not yet aware of research demonstrating that AI can be as effective. Please examine your choices and choose wisely if you seek support solely from an AI resource when confronted with a serious situation.

CHAPTER 24

GET ON WITH IT!

It's hard to describe the lightness of being that arrived in the months and early years after I stopped drinking for the second time in my life. After having been sober for a year, I could see that my drinking had completely clouded my vision.

About to turn fifty years old, I had lost sight of the dream that first emerged in my mid-thirties—that I would devote myself to helping others find meaning in their work as I had found the meaning in my own.

I knew from working with hundreds of Vertex colleagues along the way that a fulfilling work life was much more about how we choose to see our work than it is about the work itself. And with a clearer perspective, I began to see again how interchangeable our paths were.

The meaning I experienced at work was intertwined with others at Vertex, enriching the overall experience for all of us. While certainly the emphasis was different for each of us, the reality was that to fully experience the meaning that mattered to us, we needed willing colleagues with whom to share that meaning.

Reenergized by clearing the clouds from my brain, I started to see that the organization and I were ready for a change. I was slowly coming to grips with the reality that sooner or later the time would come to say goodbye to a business and a role that meant so much more to me than just a job.

In my heart of hearts, I desperately held on to hope that the failing strategy would experience a breakthrough, and I could leave a hero, fulfilling the vision of meaningful global impact that we'd created twenty years before. Letting go for me was never easy, and this was no exception.

Rarely did Rich offer me direct guidance. But when he saw me hesitating, he looked me right in the eye and said, "Get on with it, Jeff. You've done enough." He could see that I was stuck, and he had the wisdom to know that the time had come when I needed his help.

He also knew that for the good of all stakeholders, any further elongation of the successor cultivation phase would be damaging. And that meant I had to finally commit to retiring from the company I loved. After our conversation, I let the board know that I was ready to set a date.

It was the right thing to do for the good of my health, my family, the company, and all the people who depended on it. Yet again, I needed help to see the situation as it was and to do the next right thing to fulfill my aspiration to be of service to those who had been so gracious in their service to me.

At our October 2016 Vertex customer conference, I announced to our employees, customers, and partners that nearly twenty years at the helm was enough for anyone and it was time for me to move on.

REFLECTION

The experience of letting go deepened my gratitude and appreciation for my father, Jim Patton, Terry Kyle, and Rich Teerlink. Each had known that holding on wasn't the best way to serve the people they cared about.

My father retired in his early sixties to be closer to my mother as her health declined. Jim selflessly watched as I moved on from his mentorship to prove to myself that I could navigate without his hand on my shoulder. After the sale of SMS, Terry clearly could have joined another company as its CFO or CEO and expanded his impressive resume, but he chose to put his health and family ahead of more money and prestige.

When Rich retired as chairman and CEO of Harley-Davidson, he was approaching sixty-five. Fifteen years later, when he told me in no uncertain terms, "Get on with it, Jeff," I was approaching fifty-five and he was approaching eighty.

Now that I'm sixty-four, I can appreciate his wisdom so much more. The Harley board had made it clear to him that he was welcome to remain as CEO for at least five more years, but he stepped down with the foresight that it wasn't healthy for any enterprise to become identified with its leader.

Rich knew that my transition and pursuit of my life's work—helping others find their life's work—was going to take time and energy. More than that, he knew that the road ahead was going to be very different from the one I had traveled to that point. It was clearly time to get on with it, and he provided the nudge I needed to take the next step.

This was a path I was honored to follow with the sense that I would be moving toward something that held even greater promise. Yes, the road ahead was unknowable, beyond my comfort zone, but I was confident that things would work out.

A meaningful dream of a better tomorrow, of making a difference in some meaningful way, is a powerful thing. It can give us the courage to accept the necessary risk of growth, to let go of what holds us back, and to embrace the hope and promise of a better future.

Fueled by the dream and encouraged by a loving mentor, we put plans for my transition from my long-held CEO role into motion. My successor was chosen, and the transition was made smoothly.

ACTION STEPS—LETTING GO!

So many of us become stuck in our comfort zones, unable to move forward and create something better for ourselves and those around us. These comfort zones usually aren't that comfortable at all. But we often don't move on because the comfort of the known feels safer than the risk of the unknown.

Taking an inventory of your work life and taking stock of what's working and what's not is a great way to determine what you need to let go of in support of your journey and vision of a new work life.

This isn't meant as an argument for changing employers for the sake of it, something many of us do only to find ourselves deeply disappointed. It is an argument for considering a change in how you think and feel about your current work life experience and making sure your actions line up with your intent.

Here are some simple steps to help you regularly take stock in the spirit of creating a more meaningful and fulfilling future work life. Anyone can do this with only a modest amount of help from a caring friend, colleague, or guide.

1. Describe your current work life, emphasizing what is meaningful to you about it and what you wouldn't want to lose as you look ahead, as well as what you would like to change.

2. Brainstorm a list of key strategies and actions that are important to realize this better future work life. Ask yourself, "What do I need to *stop* doing, *start* doing, and *continue* doing to realize change?" Capture your thinking without judgment.

3. Wait a few days and revisit the list and make any refinements or changes. As you can see, the *letting go* part starts with a clear understanding of what you must stop doing. The beauty of this process is that it also opens up space for the change you seek by defining what you need to start doing.

4. Invite a friend, colleague, or guide, someone whose only interest is your well-being, to listen as you share your stop-start-continue list with them. Ask them for feedback and perspective.

5. Revisit your list regularly so you build this muscle and it becomes easier and easier to flex. The key is making sure these positive changes in your life align with your long-term goals and vision for a better work life.

AI NOTE: AI can be a wonderful partner in helping you imagine and understand the possibilities for your future work life if and when you emerge from a painful change in your work life reality. As always, you are the only true source of your own answers. However, like reading this book, AI can provide enormously helpful insight that can inform the choices you are about to make.

A BEGINNER'S MIND

In my late twenties and early thirties, the experience of realizing how little I understood opened my eyes, and my heart, to a sense of wonder about what else I would learn.

What I didn't know, and couldn't know, was how hard it would be to try to live and lead Vertex from the beliefs and principles that had emerged during my period of exploration. I had discovered a new mountain and committed myself to reaching the summit with no mountain-climbing experience and without so much as a compass.

The going would be tough and the lessons would be hard. Thankfully, I had guides at my side, encouraging me and giving me confidence that they wouldn't let me fall off a cliff and that I could make it if I stuck with it.

We have all heard at one time or another that experience is the greatest teacher. What we haven't heard is that there is no shortcut for getting that experience. Sure, we can skip through the training film, and we can use AI to speed the research and drafting process, but we can't fast-forward the development of self-awareness, real knowledge, true wisdom, and trusting relationships.

These can only be forged the hard way.

And it is a hard way. It's so hard that many people simply fold up the tents and give up on the idea that work could be anything more than a dreary slog with little or no hope of appreciation and not even a glimmer of true meaning.

What's worse, many sit in their unhappiness, convinced that the problem is the boss, the company, the work, or the world, never realizing that they have the key to their own fulfillment, regardless of the external forces beyond their control.

As my early inspiration gave way to the hard slog, I often lost sight of the summit that had inspired me in the first place. It seemed so far away, and the trail toward it had so many ravines and dark places. I found myself wondering why I wasn't more joyful and happy on this journey.

Slowly I came to understand that meaningfulness and happiness are two very different things. If something matters enough to us, we'll suffer tremendous hardship, risk, and even pain to see it through. Much of that effort would never fit into our definition of happiness. Suffering is not fun, and it's definitely not joyful.

I look back on my martial arts training and learning how to break a slab of concrete with my bare palm. It took years of intensive training, and yes, it was, quite literally, a painful process. Today, I take pride in having achieved my black belt, breaking that concrete slab (and nearly my arm).

While I was never going to be a tae kwon do master, I proved to myself that I could become something more than I was before. But getting there was at times a slog, and without the discipline and support of my guides and the help of my colleagues, I couldn't have made much real progress.

The big lesson of the long journey from inspiration to achievement was simply this: Meaning is not happiness, it's not easy, and there is no shortcut to it. A working life of meaning, and the fulfillment to draw from it, is a long, hard climb.

And sometimes when you achieve success, an even bigger hurdle emerges—starting to believe you know all you need to know, or that because you are successful you should be happy.

Whenever I began to think I knew it all, the universe found even bigger hurdles to throw in my path, reminding me that whatever mountain I thought I had successfully climbed, there was another, much more challenging mountain waiting on the other side.

Master Kwon, my martial arts teacher, and an eighth-degree tae kwon do grand master, would often say to me, like a drill sergeant with a Korean accent, "Remember, Jeff, beginner's mind!" I would step back, take a breath, clear my head, and start over again with my training.

We are never through learning and growing. Staying open, curious, and eager to learn is crucial to understanding that every challenge is an opportunity to learn and to create meaning. Sometimes the journey may be devoid of happiness, but along the way, it's possible to experience a kind of fulfillment that is much more rewarding.

ACTING

EASY PEASY

In my mid-thirties, I began to imagine a life after Vertex where I would contribute what I could to the movement toward more meaningful work. In my mid-fifties, after I accepted Rich's challenge to get on with it, I was finally able to let go of the role that had defined not only my career but my life.

I was free to embrace the vision that had been percolating within me for years. The time had come to write the book, hit the speaker's circuit, and do what I could to help illuminate the interconnectedness of all work. I could see that my twenty-eight years as an employee was really preparation for what I saw as my true calling: speaking the gospel of meaningful and fulfilling work for anyone who wanted it!

I had spent a few hours here and there jotting down some of the key ideas that would animate my message. I also spoke to a handful of student groups to test whether the message had traction. I wasn't surprised to find the same response from nearly everyone I spoke with: "Hmmm. I've never thought about that. The meaning of my work?"

It was gratifying to watch the light bulbs flash on when people connected the dots and began to understand that every time they buy a cup of coffee at Dunkin' Donuts, they are triggering a massive network of technology, including the tax calculation that makes that purchase possible. It reminded me that I had a role to play in shining a light on a massive blind spot that robs millions of workers from the awareness that their efforts matter so much more than the company bottom line.

Maybe sharing the real-world lessons from my own experience could help people navigate the uncertain and unpredictable journey toward a work life that matters. All I had to do now was write the book, practice my public speaking, and hit the road. Easy peasy!

Or so I thought.

WHY WRITE A BOOK?

"What's the purpose of the book?" Rich asked.

We were walking along the Milwaukee waterfront on a glorious spring afternoon in 2016, about six months before my retirement as CEO would become official. He had asked me if I was going to move forward with my plans to author a book about my journey and the insights about the meaning of business that had emerged for me along the way.

I looked at him and saw that even at eighty, he had that same mischievous twinkle in his eye that told me there was something powerful he was wanting me to discover. Some insight lying just beneath the surface of his seemingly simple question.

Aware of the loving challenge he was offering, I pondered his question as we walked in silence. The sun sparkled off the metallic trim of the office buildings rising up before us and glinted off the gentle ripples in the lake to our left, virtually blinding me as we walked.

Time stood still in that moment. Rich's tenure as a Vertex board member had come to a close a year before, and it was becoming increasingly clear to me that his memory and mental abilities were showing the signs of something more than old age. I had a strong sense that my hours of meaningful reflection and philosophical exploration with my second remarkable mentor were soon to draw to a close.

I wanted to savor the moment and hold on to it for the rest of my days. Who was I to have this privileged tutelage from a corporate legend in the waning years of his long and remarkable work life? Surely there had to be a reason.

Both Jim and Rich had taught me that change happens when the learner's desire for more knowledge comes from their own sense of deep personal commitment. They helped me realize that when there is a process of ongoing trial, error, and reflection, fueled by an internal yearning to grow, that's when real learning and real growth happens.

Reflecting on those hard-won discoveries, I looked back at Rich, feeling a wave of gratitude roll over me. I said, simply, "Thank you." And then I asked myself, *What IS the point of writing a book?*

A book alone is an event, a single experience at a single point in time. An inspiring speech to introduce the book is also a single event. The learning opportunity from an event is meaningful, but it fades. Books like Covey's *7 Habits* can be life changing, but without the experience of applying their lessons with the support of a wise guide, would they have led me to sustainable change?

Only through repeated exposure, genuine striving, and real consequences over time did any new awareness take hold in my work life. Events like reading a book or hearing a speech served as useful invitations to expand my existing experiences. Without the ideas in those books and lectures as prompts, I wouldn't have taken the first steps toward real progress and change. Even though books and speeches can't, by their very nature, interact with my real world of work and my inner journey, they have been the sparks that lit the flame of my drive for change and improvement. They started me on my own personal journey of loss, struggle, success, and failure. I hope my book does that for you.

It became clear to me that for people to translate ideas into meaningful change they needed sustained effort and experience, with many failures, like I had experienced over my career and Rich had in his. There weren't any shortcuts for Rich and me; why should we expect others to grasp the deeper meaning of work solely from reading a book?

We walked a bit farther, and I told him about attending Peter Senge's speech at Drexel University many years before. At the time, I was blown away by what he had done. Over a thousand people had gathered to hear the famed MIT professor and author of *The Fifth Discipline* share his wisdom with the vague expectation that doing so would magically unlock the hidden potential in their careers.

Senge spoke for no more than thirty minutes. For the rest of the two hours, he challenged the audience to share perspectives with each other in small groups. He offered only a few provocative questions to guide the dialogue. Senge's message was clear: You won't find the wisdom you need from the guy behind the podium. You will find it only in your own heart and amid your own real struggle, with the help of those around you. Anything else is at best fleeting inspiration, or if you're lucky, a glimpse of something previously undiscovered.

Senge, Covey, Jaworski, and others were sparks. Their books and their words led me to have hundreds of meaningful conversations that ultimately allowed me to test their ideas in the real world, validating them through hard-won experience.

As I continued walking with Rich, I had a flash of intuitive insight. I realized that my hope was that my book would inspire people who are ready to make a change to start practicing and developing their own inner strength. My insight was that the book was just the start. It, alone, was not all I was called to do. I said, "OK, Rich, I got it. I need to create a space where people can support each other through their real experiences. That process has to begin wherever that person wants to start, on their terms, not mine."

He just smiled that knowing smile, eyes twinkling in the resplendent sunshine. I felt like I was suspended in time and space, as though not a minute had passed, and we hadn't walked a single step. In reality, we had walked close to a mile, and my watch said we had been together for over an hour.

Rich helped me to remember that I needed to apply my learning to my true purpose—to enable anyone to see the meaning of their work. The passion unleashed by that awareness would not only benefit those who sought it, but if it were to catch on, could also inspire a new level of contribution to the well-being of all.

With a single question, Rich had elevated a vision that had been bubbling within me for decades. The problem was that I had no idea how I was going to do anything about it!

I left Milwaukee that evening confident that I knew what I needed to do, and why, but with no idea how. I was also confident that the same synchronicity that had led me to Rich in the first place would lead me to exactly what I would need, and exactly when I would need it, for my continuing journey.

I was ready to close the door on my career as a CEO and open the door to my true calling.

REFLECTION

Some of the greatest gifts arrive in ugly wrapping paper, and some arrive in perfect moments like the glorious afternoon in Milwaukee with Rich. Some arrive in the middle of the night, and others while driving through the mountains of north-central Pennsylvania on a perfect fall afternoon.

I don't know when they'll happen, but I know that when they do, they will be unmistakable. These gifts are moments of clarity that are so perfect that I know in an instant they are exactly what is needed at exactly the moment they are needed. What makes these inspirational insights so different is they represent a leap that I could not have imagined through analytical thought or mechanical calculation.

I don't know how to bring them about, only that they tend to happen when I am not thinking or trying to solve the problem. Having had this happen many times, I am thoroughly convinced, as are my guides who have all experienced this sense of intuitive leap, that this kind of insight is available to anyone. I am no expert in the science of mind, but the actual experts advise that the primary condition to have such experiences is to simply be open to them and recognize them when they happen.

School does not train us to access our ability to cultivate and recognize intuitive insight. School trains us on how to remember information, analyze and solve problems correctly, and develop useful skills. These are all highly valuable abilities. The problem is that without efforts to develop our naturally given intuitive abilities, the more analytical and functional activities that are schooled into us tend to crowd out our more subtle and creative capacities.

For many of us, it has been so long since we experienced creative intuition that we've forgotten what it feels like. The good news is we can revive these abilities with willingness and some simple practices.

ACTION STEPS—CULTIVATING INTUITIVE INSIGHT

Peter Senge's speech was a spark. His goal was to get the audience to engage in meaningful conversations and make connections that they otherwise wouldn't have made.

That is my goal with these action steps—to spark your intuitive thinking and for you to have those meaningful conversations. Here are five simple steps to cultivate your natural ability to attract intuitive insight.

1. Unlike a math problem or a new skill like hitting a golf ball, intuitive insight isn't subject to the laws of physical or intellectual development through repetitive training. And it can't be simply turned on when it's time for "intuition training" any more than one could turn on true love at an appointed date and hour. Step 1 is to recognize that intuition happens, but it cannot be *made* to happen.

2. Because all of us do have real challenges and have real intuitive abilities, whether we are aware of them or not, we can reflect on our past experiences to see where we have experienced our intuition. That reflection will help us better cultivate the context for future intuitive insights. Step 2 is to go for a walk in a park or otherwise get away from a desk and technology. Look back over your career thus far, or your life pre-career. Do you recall a moment when you suddenly just knew what you needed to do?

3. When you return to your workspace, jot down all the thoughts that came up for you, even the ones that don't seem in any way relevant to creative intuition. With your notes in front of you, consider this question: What were the circumstances surrounding your moment of knowing? Where were you? What was happening? Who were you with? Why was the moment of knowing so memorable?

4. Reflect on what you've learned. Consider the challenges, opportunities, fears, and passions you have today and remind yourself that these aren't math problems and they can't be solved in the same way. Find opportunities to create the kind of context that you experienced in the past when moments of knowing happened. Every time you sense something creative,

insightful, or intuitive, jot it down along with the context around which it happened. Every few months or so, share your experiences with a friend, colleague, or guide.

AI NOTE: The ability of AI to draw upon vast stores of information and synthesize that information at a scale and speed never before experienced by people and then present the essence of this analysis in plain language that sounds just like you can feel very much like the kind of insight I have just described. And, that kind of synthesis can expand your own sense of the possible, a key element of attracting intuitive insight. At the same time, AI can't process your feelings and beliefs, your expressed and yet to be expressed aspirations and fears, or those of the people you care about. But it can present you an opportunity that is so profoundly beyond what you could have imagined as to feel almost miraculous. AI can help, but the insight must ultimately emerge from within you!

CHAPTER 26

A SPHERE IS BORN

"**B**ubba! Hey, Bubba, come here!" I bellowed.

It was February 2017 and we were floating on a sailboat off a deserted atoll in the middle of the Indian Ocean. I was shouting to Jen, who had been affectionately known as Bubba since we were dating.

In celebration of my retirement, we had been taking a long sailing trip down a chain of atolls in the Indian Ocean known as the Maldives. I had purposefully held off on trying to do much actual writing of this book until my corporate duties had been formally completed the previous October, and thus far I had managed to scratch out only a dozen pages of rough ideas.

At this point in our travels, we had put a good distance between ourselves and the rest of humanity. Anchored beside an uninhabited atoll two thousand miles from any significant human population, surrounded by nothing but ocean, sand, palm trees, and coral reefs, it was the perfect setting to ponder the meaning of my work life experience and to begin working on this book in earnest. My walk with Rich in Milwaukee was still fresh in the back of my mind.

Jen arrived. She could tell something was up by the look on my face. "What's going on?"

"Bubba, check this out!"

Sitting in the shade with my iPad, I had been playing around with a simple software tool that produces visual diagrams. I had the vague idea that these diagrams would help readers connect what each person does at work to the greater benefit of that work.

So much of what we do, like the sales tax software I'd spent a career advancing, was buried deeply within the products and services that actually touch people's lives—like the cars we drive or food we eat. How could I help people see the myriad connections and understand their importance?

I was having a ball experimenting with all these various connections and networks in my work, life, and career when something clicked. It was similar to what had happened to me on that drive home through the mountains of Pennsylvania on a fall day almost twenty years earlier. Rather than start with me and my relationships at the center of the rough little diagram before me, and rather than start with Vertex and its clients at the center, I thought, *What is actually at the center of it all?* After a moment, I started a new diagram with one word in the middle: meaning.

Like the intuitive click, the next question came *through* me. The simple question was: What do most people find meaningful? That simple question led to a burst of inspiration that I tried to capture in little bubbles.

Safety—Joy—Love—Fun—Connection—Wellness—Significance.

That's when I fully realized that every single thing we do is ultimately an effort to experience one or more of these feelings or sensations. We all want more love, more joy, more safety, more nourishment, more connection, more insight, more fun, more convenience, more contribution to others, or more significance. Even if we think what we want is more money, we only want more money so we can get more of one of these essential states of being.

Jen squinted and leaned in to study what I'd been writing.

As I thought about it, it seemed evident that all of human endeavor is in service to these basic, eternal, and ubiquitous needs. The pursuit of meeting these needs is what gives meaning to our lives.

- Watch a beautiful sunset? Feel more joy.
- Go to the gym and exercise? Feel more alive.
- Get married? Feel more love.
- Buy a smartphone? Feel more connected.
- Care for a child? Feel more fulfilled.

These are the things that move us to action because they are deeply and intrinsically meaningful to us. It occurred to me that all human effort, including all business effort, must ultimately serve this short list of eternally meaningful feelings.

Upon further reflection, it dawned on me that being part of helping others achieve these states of being gave us perhaps the most significant meaning of all—a feeling of having significance, of having mattered by having served another's sense of worth, dignity, and growth. And I noticed that none of the most meaningful things on my list were *things* at all. They were all feelings!

It then occurred to me that while every business delivers something toward these ultimate ends, the biggest businesses deliver the most visible and far-reaching impact, often combining hundreds or thousands of other contributions from other businesses into massively complex systems that enable humanity to achieve truly miraculous experiences.

With these observations bouncing around my head and through my entire being, the little diagram before me grew exponentially. I started from the very idea that at our core we are continual meaning-makers, striving to achieve the experiences that create deeper and richer meaning in our lives. As I connected more and more entities with the essential elements of meaning surrounding the word "meaning" at the center, the model grew to ultimately connect all kinds of massive organizations and the products they create to the contribution of the people who create them. The resulting model linked everything together from "Meaning" in the center to "File Tax Returns" at the outer edge, with "Build Cars" and "Create Connections" in between.

"Bubba, it's a diagram of all businesses, connected to all of the most meaningful things people are ultimately wanting, with the very notion of meaning at the center of it all!" I exclaimed, transfixed and proud.

"Geez! What do you call that thing?" she asked. She stared at the screen in front of me, half curious, half perplexed.

I had to think about that for a minute. While the model in front of me was flat and two dimensional, it formed a rough circle. After staring at it for a few moments I realized that ultimately, if it were to be fully populated, it would have to be three-dimensional like a globe or sphere.

"It's a sphere of meaning," I told her.

"I get it. And that's super cool, honey, but it doesn't exactly roll off the tongue," she said, helpfully.

She headed back to her spot in the sun, immediately immersed again in planning for her next film. I continued to ponder the notion of helping anyone, anywhere, see how their work actually contributed, in some small way, to the entirety of our human experience.

With the sage input of my partner for life, I kept rearranging the words and landed on the name MeaningSphere. And no, it still didn't roll off the tongue. But neither did "Google" until Google became, well, Google.

It was then that I realized what Rich had been challenging me to discover when he asked me, "What's the purpose of the book?" I could now see that no book alone could provide the support, perspective, interaction, community, and mentoring that people, like me, needed, along with time and experience, to see the meaningful connections in their own work lives.

The big click was unmistakable. I could see that what was needed was an interactive platform and community where people could access others seeking meaning in their careers, mentors to guide them on their journey, and resources to help them make their work lives meaningful. And I knew that was what I was meant to do.

I sat there soaking in the simple insight. Books had helped me immensely. They sparked a fire in me. But without continuous support from Jim, Terry, Rich, and others, and without tools like the Covey survey, I wouldn't have been able to create so much meaning out of a career in something as seemingly mundane as tax software. In that moment I resolved to apply my unique business experience and remarkable resources to create a platform that could help anyone have the experience that I'd had—but for a fraction of the cost.

And that's how my new venture, the MeaningSphere, was born. The only witnesses were Jen and me on a lovely little island in the Indian Ocean. As I sat there staring out over the endless reefs and atolls, I was filled with a new hope and vision of a world where every job was infused with a sense of meaning—unleashing creativity, innovation, prosperity, and wellness the world over.

REFLECTION

Yes, this really happened just as described here. No, you don't need to have some world-changing epiphany to have a work life of your dreams. We all have unique roles to play in creating the world of the future, one sales tax calculation at a time.

And no, you don't have to have the resources to travel to the farthest points on the planet to find inspiration. My first aha moment was driving a Ford F-150 pickup, which was also our family car, down a local road in the northern tier of Pennsylvania coal country. Your nearest state or local park is more than sufficient access to natural surroundings to support your own meaning-making.

Looking back to my childhood, the first experience I ever had of a "moment of knowing" was when I was about twelve. I was standing in the garage sanding the edges of a seven-foot-long wooden rowboat that my father and I were building together.

He had left me unsupervised after pointing to a spot about a foot ahead of where I was, saying, "You can stop there." When I had progressed to that point, I paused, proud of my work. Out of nowhere it occurred to me to just go ahead without his permission and finish that whole side of the little boat, another five feet!

When he saw what I had done, well, it was probably the first time I thought my father was actually proud of me. Only now can I fully appreciate how that single moment set the course of my entire life.

In reflection, my point is this: We all have abilities beyond whatever was taught to us in school that can inspire us to take on all kinds of challenges, large and small, simple, and complex, guiding us toward truly meaningful outcomes.

Your work life is infused with the potential to contribute something deeply meaningful to you, to others, and to the whole of humanity. And you don't need anyone's permission to try. As my friend, mentor, colleague, and author of the book *I Give Myself Permission*, Dr. George James, said to me, "You are free to give yourself permission today to become the person you want to be."*

---

* George James, personal communication with author, January 2026.

ACTION STEPS—CREATING THE WORK LIFE OF YOUR DREAMS

Whatever your work is, there is likely more meaning in it than you may currently realize. That meaning—the meaning that actually matters to you—can only be created by you. The choice is yours.

You are certainly free to keep doing what you are doing and wait to see what happens. Or, if you want a more satisfying and ultimately fulfilling work life, you can create the work life of your dreams. You don't need anyone's permission, but you may need the support of a caring friend, colleague, or guide and perhaps a boost from artificial intelligence, where appropriate.

Here are the steps:

1. What do you find meaningful about the work you are currently doing? Jot down your observations.

2. Head to your go-to place for creative thinking. Once settled and away from distractions, imagine your future ten or more years out. I suggest doing this, as it helps get beyond the "what next" habit that is ingrained in us from an early age, and it energizes our creative flow.

3. As you imagine, let your mind wander. Try to avoid solving the problem or analyzing the situation. Just allow your mind to wander, imagining what your ideal future work life would look like and feel like. Jot down your thoughts. If you feel like it, draw simple pictures, whether you have any artistic ability or not!

4. How do you feel as you engage in this experience? Awkward? Joyful? Weird? Scared? Excited? Observe your feelings and jot them down.

5. Repeat this process as much as you feel a desire to do so. For some, a significant sense of clarity may occur on the very first

try; for others, many months may go by without even a hint of inspiration. Beware, your practice may cause the inspiration to rise up in you when you least expect it!

AI NOTE: Once you have an insight about, or vision of, your ten-year dream work life, you can use AI to help express that dream in the form of a mural or other visual depiction of what the dream means to you. For some, it might be a sunrise; for others, a spreadsheet drawn across a mountain. Whatever images best reflect the essence of your work life ideal, ask AI to help you portray them visually. Or, if you feel comfortable, go the old-fashioned way and just draw. Stick figures are cool!

CHAPTER 27

SYNCHRONICITY AT YOUR SERVICE!

"**F**olks, I just want to take a second to welcome a special guest."

Speaking was John Mackey, the cofounder and CEO of Whole Foods Market, which he had recently sold to Amazon. He was presiding over the 2017 Conscious Capitalism CEO Summit, and I was among the 250 or so people in attendance in Austin, Texas. I was joining the group for the first time, just as my retirement as CEO was official.

Mackey earned his iconic status the hard way, building Whole Foods up from its earliest days as a hippie-style natural food market in Austin to ultimately become the pacesetter for an entire movement toward healthier eating and living. Having carefully nurtured the tiny flame of his massive vision into an iconic brand, my ears perked up when he mentioned a special guest.

"Please welcome my good friend and the author of *Synchronicity*, Joseph Jaworski," Mackey said.

My head just about exploded. Two decades earlier, Jim Patton had given me a copy of Joseph's book. I had devoured it immediately. In the book, Jaworski described his remarkable journey to realizing that his intentional thinking and search for meaning opened doors for him that he could not have opened on his own. The book described the kind of experience I went on to have as I worked with Rich Teerlink, Terry Kyle, and so many of the remarkable people who would make my own journey so meaningful, enabling me to better serve my own purpose.

There I sat in the audience, not seeking to meet anyone in particular. I had no expectation that this person, who had had such an impact on my career, would simply appear as if by magic in the back of the room. He had no role in the conference. Mackey simply felt that his presence as a visitor that day was worth mentioning to those in attendance.

The shortest possible version of Joseph's story is that as a young man he found himself in the middle of the emergency search for victims of a massive tornado in Waco, Texas. During a twenty-four-hour period, he worked side by side with people he had never known and would never meet again, sorting through the rubble left by the tornado, searching for the living buried below.

The experience was transformative for Joseph. He felt both exhausted and lighter than air, as though connected to everything and everyone around him. His experience was just like the one I had that fall day in the Pennsylvania mountains.

Joseph couldn't come up with words to describe his experience at twenty years of age, but he later realized that he had touched upon something remarkable. He spent the rest of his career searching for the secret to achieving that special state of flow, where incredible effort feels incredibly effortless.

The son of famed Watergate special prosecutor Leon Jaworski, Joseph first went into the legal profession himself, helping to build a storied firm and developing a powerful practice of his own. He was elected as a fellow of the American College of Trial Lawyers in 1975, an honor awarded to the top 1 percent of American litigators.

But the experience of Waco was always in the back of his mind. Against the wishes and expectations of his father and partners, he left the law, determined to bring that sense of inspired flow to business leaders everywhere and to apply what he learned to some of the largest challenges facing humanity.

In 1980, Jaworski founded the American Leadership Forum, a nongovernmental organization dedicated to strengthening collaborative civic leadership in the United States. He later joined the Royal Dutch/Shell Group of companies in London to head Shell's renowned team of scenario planners. Under his leadership, the Shell team made a fundamental shift in the way the company framed and used scenarios as a tool for strategy formation.

At the conference in Austin, at the first break in the action, I practically ran to the back of the room in search of this man who had changed my life by sharing his remarkable experiences through his books. As soon as I caught his attention, I said, "Joseph, my name is Jeff Westphal, and I am one of those guys who comes up to you and says, 'Your book changed my life.'"

He just smiled, chuckling.

"Will you spend an afternoon with me, anywhere, anytime?" I spit it out like I was a teenager and had just asked LeBron James to play a game of one-on-one.

"I would be delighted," he replied.

That is the story of the synchronicity that led me to meet the author of the book *Synchronicity*. Joseph and I met and continued to work together on a biweekly basis for the next three years as I sought insight into my new role as Vertex board chairperson and in my journey to nurture the MeaningSphere into existence.

Rich's journey into the depths of dementia made it increasingly difficult for him to provide the unwavering support to which I had become accustomed. His decline provided me with the opportunity to honor him by showing up for him in Milwaukee as he had shown up for me in Philadelphia. Having tried to be present for both Jim and my father as each navigated the journey through dementia, I had a strong understanding of what the years ahead held for Rich and his beloved wife, Ann.

I knew I needed a new mentor and trusted that the right person would appear at the right time and in the right way, just as I had come to meet Jim, Terry, and Rich.

Joseph and his business partner, Susan Taylor, took up the mentorship baton. They helped me stay the course as I worked to nourish MeaningSphere into being.

REFLECTION

And there it was again. The pattern was undeniable. At no point over nearly thirty years had I gone out looking for a mentor or coach. And here I was, yet again, staring at exactly the right person, at exactly the right moment, to help me act on the purpose growing within me.

In *Synchronicity*, Joseph summarizes the work of leading philosophers and physicists to illuminate the fundamental idea that our intentions have a strange ability to attract what we need when we need it. This includes people who challenge us and support us on our various paths through life, including work.

Joseph had come across an article in the newspaper about a quantum physicist named David Bohm. Seizing the moment of creative inspiration, he reached out to Bohm and practically begged to meet him. It was that initial meeting and successive meetings with other leading thinkers that inspired him to write *Synchronicity*.

Just like the creative inspirations that come to us seemingly out of nowhere, the coincidences that are too remarkable to be coincidences point us in the direction of our purpose.

To further illustrate the point, about six months before I introduced myself to Joseph Jaworski, I had accidentally met a woman named Betty Sue Flowers. As it turns out, Betty Sue had been the editor of *Synchronicity*.

At no point did Betty Sue ever suggest an introduction to Joseph, and it never dawned on me to ask her for one. And yet there I was six months later, shaking hands with the man whose writing had helped me trust that forces larger than myself would guide me to what I needed. How else can I explain having met so many important mentors from Bill North to Betty Sue Flowers without even seeking to meet anyone?

Step up to the universe buffet! You never know when you might get a heaping serving of synchronicity.

ACTION STEPS—ATTRACTING THE SUPERPOWER OF SYNCHRONICITY

It wouldn't be synchronicity if you could plan, schedule, or buy it. It only happens when you have a sense of purpose and are paying attention to its possibilities. Synchronicity is happening all the time for all kinds of people with all kinds of passions and purposes.

Most of us, like me, don't even recognize it; if we do, we write it off to coincidence and nothing more. That's what would have happened in my work life if Joseph hadn't authored the book and Jim hadn't given the book to me to read.

Once I was aware of it, I could start to see it happening. That's why I went to Harley-Davidson. I didn't know that I was going to meet the CEO who would become my second mentor. A door had opened, seemingly by accident, when the Harley executive invited me to visit him at the York plant, and the rest unfolded naturally from there.

The same thing happened when a long-term Vertex colleague, Linda Macaleer, said to me one day that her father had noticed our success and would enjoy meeting me. Her father happened to be the founder of SMS, one of the leading software firms in the Philadelphia area at the time.

Sensing a door opening, I reached out and had lunch with him. The lunch led to an introduction to none other than Terry Kyle, SMS's recently retired CFO. He became the essential coach and mentor we would need to help Vertex get to the next level.

Here are five simple steps you can take to attract synchronicities to help you serve your work life purpose:

1. Review your dream work life. Does it still lift your spirits? Do you still feel inspired by it, no matter how difficult it may seem to achieve? If not, refresh your effort until you feel inspired! (If not you, who? If not now, when?)

2. Reflect on your career journey to this point. Review all the events and relationships that have led you to where you are now. Identify the connections, events, and surprises that couldn't have been planned but without which you wouldn't be where you are now.

3. Consider that the path from where you are to your dream work life isn't a straight line. Has your life and career been a straight line so far? Why would you expect it to be a straight line in the future? Imagine a winding path, full of big leaps and difficult challenges, helping you gain new awareness, strength, and the knowledge necessary to realize your dreams.

4. Take a walk in your favorite natural setting and let yourself imagine the work life that would be most meaningful for you. Why is it meaningful? How will you feel when you are living that work life? Why will you feel that way? Allow yourself to simply hold those ideas in your mind, without doing anything about them but imagining them becoming your future reality.

5. Ask a friend, colleague, or guide to spend some time with you. Share your aspirations. Continue to do this every few months as you pay attention to the developments around you and within you. Share your observations with your colleague.

6. As you move forward in your work life, pay attention to new people, opportunities, and challenges that emerge, seemingly out of nowhere. Ask yourself, Why has this person or event come into my work life? Could there be more significance to this than initially meets the eye? Be patient, stay awake, and act on your intuition!

AI NOTE: This experience is about paying attention to developments in your work life that may not have seemed significant upon first observation. It's about being wide awake to what is happening around and within you. This is not an AI-assisted exercise.

CHAPTER 28

THE ROAD TO MEANINGSPHERE

After Jen and I returned from the Maldives, it was time for action. I knew that creating a place for anyone, anywhere to create more meaning and gain more fulfillment from the work they do would require a team of collaborators who shared my values and had the experience and skills that would complement my own.

Soon after our return, Alex Smith, Keith Lewish, and Jory Tremblay joined me as cofounders of MeaningSphere. The following year, Dr. Theresa Bolmarcich created a market study to test my assumptions about the prevalence of meaning-aware workers in the United States. And soon after that, Dr. Hadley Williams helped us clarify and professionalize our designs.

Each brought a set of experiences to our creative effort that added a dimension that I knew we would need to turn a dream into reality. More than tangible skills and knowledge, each possessed a way of being that I knew from my years at Vertex would help contribute richness to our collaborations. Vision, story, analysis, strategy, rigor, detail, and concept were all as important as communications, psychology, research, finance, tech, operations, and marketing.

The core leadership team of Keith, Jory, Alex, and I began slowly and intentionally meeting every two weeks to shape the original vision into a strategy. We were all either semiretired or nearly so. None of us needed or wanted a job, and we all agreed that if we were going to do this, we wanted to create something that could have a major positive benefit to the movement toward more meaningful work that we believed was already underway.

Our research showed a growing community of outstanding thought leaders in the arena, and there wasn't much that we could add to their scholarship or their ability to convey the central ideas that had animated our efforts at Vertex for twenty years. Simon Sinek, Brené Brown, Adam Grant, and Daniel Pink, among many others, were adding a more modern flavor to the ideas that were developed by the founders of the movement. Douglas McGregor, Stephen Covey, Peter Senge, Meg Wheatley, Ken Blanchard, and Joseph Jaworski had each contributed a unique element to the growing body of knowledge and experience about the power of people, relationships, purpose, and inspiration in the workplace.

MeaningSphere wasn't to be the impetus for the movement. But it could be the vehicle to help the movement scale.

Our road to MeaningSphere was reasonably smooth until 2019, when the pandemic hit. By then we had incorporated and carried out foundational research upon which to ground our beliefs about the nature of the market, the need, and the individuals we sought to serve. We had attracted our first few full-time colleagues and were creating the first conceptual versions of the platform. Working virtually, it wasn't terribly difficult to sustain our efforts while the pandemic, and its uncertainties, swirled around us.

We had real momentum, with a growing cadre of about a dozen

full- and part-time collaborators, when we experienced several shocks to our system. We sustained one hit after the other.

First, the crash of the tech stock market put a severe strain on my ability to sustain funding through the summer of 2022. This led to a brave effort by our crew to keep going. Many worked without full pay for a few months that summer, and we reduced the number of positions available to preserve cash. This delayed our development program.

Then we discovered that our third-party development platform did not possess the depth of information security capability that it had been represented as having. After making urgent efforts to fully meet all international compliance requirements, we concluded that we would need to adopt an entirely new platform to create the rigorously compliant security foundation we believed would be necessary to serve the mission. This transformation would require a full year.

And, just as we were emerging from that unplanned challenge, my father passed away. It was August 2023. In the months afterward, a pain that seemed to emanate from my solar plexus was radiating around to my mid-back area.

Having experienced stress-related back pain in my twenties, I assumed that I was suffering from some unresolved grief over the loss of my father. Several months went by until Jenifer finally persuaded me to go to the doctor.

"It might be stress, but it could be something physical," my doctor said. "Let's have an MRI to rule that out." After the MRI came back, she said, "We don't usually see MRIs that look quite like this. It could just be a production issue. Still, we need to run blood work to be sure."

A few days later I was in our mudroom when she called my cell phone from her vacation in Europe. "Jeff, you have multiple myeloma. The good news is it's highly treatable. You're going to be OK, but this will be a year where you need to focus primarily on the treatment plan."

The pain in my back, which by this time would flare into virtually crippling extremes, shot through my body, bringing me to my knees as she spoke. *Cancer? Me? Now? Really?* The thoughts raced through my mind.

I heard Jen walking toward me from the bedroom where she had been getting dressed. I thought as I prepared to share the news, *This is a moment that will change our lives forever.* I looked at her and said, "It's cancer. It's called multiple myeloma. It's treatable, and she says I am going to be OK." I hugged her. And we stood there, holding each other, sobbing and wondering what was to come.

The shortest version possible of this story is that everything my doctor said to me that day came to pass. After six months of immuno-therapy and a week of radiation, my cancer receded to the point where I was able to have a stem-cell transplant using my own stem cells.

Then after two weeks in the hospital sandwiched between a month of quarantine on either end, my blood quickly returned to near normal. In July, my doctor declared that I had achieved long-term remission just nine months after the original diagnosis.

For multiple myeloma, long-term remission means just that. While all patients have unique individual considerations, generally speaking, my odds of surviving fifteen-plus years are better than 85 percent. That's a pretty positive prognosis for a sixty-four-year-old with a blood-based cancer that was untreatable just twenty-five years ago.

Through the entire process, I couldn't help but be amazed by the massive array of tools and technology that saved my life. Yes, of course, the doctors, nurses, staff, and even the parking attendants were indispensable. But without the hospital itself, the treatment rooms, monitors, syringes, gauze pads, blood vials, and testing equipment, what would the doctors have been able to achieve?

The most telling moment occurred when I was lying on the radia-tion machine. This massive piece of multimillion-dollar technology was made of hundreds of parts from hundreds of businesses from all over the world. I looked up at a large glass plate and noticed that a single screw kept this massive plate in place. As I lay there awaiting the lifesaving radiation that would destroy the cancer cells that had attached themselves to my spine, giving me occasional shots of breathtaking pain, I thought, *I wonder if the people who make that screw realize that they are, in a small but critical way, helping to save my life.*

The same was true for the thousands of businesses that had created and delivered the thousands of tools and their parts that make it possible for me to live a normal life today. I now have every reason to believe that I am nearly as likely as anyone else in their mid-sixties to live a vibrant life into my eighties.

To focus on my health and make myself available for the many different medical consultations, tests, treatments, and all-important rest, I needed to reduce my work schedule by 70 percent. That meant discontinuing all sorts of engagements that had given my semiretirement meaning, in addition to cutting my involvement in MeaningSphere significantly.

Changes and advancements we needed to make that required my involvement would just have to wait.

Then another bombshell hit.

What I didn't know as I was navigating toward long-term remission and MeaningSphere was evolving toward a new normal yet again, was that the increasingly visible shake in Jenifer's left hand and the hitch in her gait was something more than the pinched nerve we assumed it must be.

Once I achieved long-term remission, Jenifer booked herself a visit to a neurologist at the urging of our doctor. It didn't take him more than one appointment to advise her that she had an early, slowly progressing form of Parkinson's disease. So, while the nascent MeaningSphere enterprise found its new normal in the fall of 2024, Jen and I began our latest journey in search of our own new normal.

What we learned soon enough is that Parkinson's disease manifests itself in very different ways in different people. While it is always progressive, meaning it gets more severe over time, the rate and type of progression vary widely from person to person.

And while there is no cure, there is a growing body of evidence that the brain can effectively bypass the damaging effects in order to sustain bodily functions much longer than previously thought possible. This emerging knowledge is broadly understood as neuroplasticity.

As MeaningSphere experimented with a soft launch of our core offering in the six months from October 2024 to March 2025, Jenifer and I experimented with what it meant to have Parkinson's disease, what neuroplasticity could make possible, and what changes in our lives would best enhance the quality of our later years.

As the formal launch of MeaningSphere approached in October 2025, we agreed that our health, our ability to live our most meaningful lives, and our ability to do our most meaningful work lay before us.

We realized how grateful we were to be surrounded by teams of wonderful, caring, capable people who could help us serve our most meaningful purposes and visions, even as we worked toward lives that provided more time for rest, walks in nature, and reduced stress.

Together, we felt we had done the heavy lifting we believed was necessary and that we could begin to enjoy the role of cheerleader for our teams who would bring our shared purposes to life at MeaningSphere; at Mosaic, a community for independent meaningful learning; at Wavelength, Jen's film company; and in our shared passion for helping revive her historic hometown of McGregor, Iowa.

REFLECTION

I now know why Rich said to me, "Get on with it" when I was fifty-five and hesitant to leave Vertex, feeling like my work there wasn't quite complete. At that time, he was eighty, and he knew that I didn't know how fast eight years could fly by in your late fifties and early sixties. He also knew that just because we had been fortunate to have never had a serious health issue until then, the sixties were different from any prior era of our lives, with different challenges.

As we've navigated through the developments of the past five years, I became highly aware that the choices that I might have made in my forties in response to these challenges would likely be different from the choices I'm making now. Had I hung on to my role as CEO, perhaps retiring from the company a few years later than I did, we wouldn't have gotten MeaningSphere far enough along before I was diagnosed with cancer to have sustained our commitment to it. It would have been a dream that was never given a chance.

When I received my diagnosis, one of my first calls was to my editor, Betty Sue. Her sage words to me were, "Jeff, don't just kick this rock out of the way. It's here to serve you."

How right she was. The entire experience made me more aware of the preciousness of life, of the action of synchronicities that shaped my experience in ways that I couldn't on my own, and of the importance of supporting the growth and independence of my colleagues so they aren't dependent on me, or any single person, to serve our shared purpose.

My cancer and Jen's Parkinson's have intensified my commitment and passion for MeaningSphere and its purpose, while at the same time lightening my heart and reducing my stress. As much as I fervently believe in the work and the people involved, cancer has reminded me in the most powerful way that I am not in control, and ultimately, what will be will be. All I can do is my best, with trust in the larger wisdom of the universe and gratitude for the opportunity to grow from what unfolds before me in the days, weeks, months, and years to come.

I feel as though I have emerged from a long, dark night of the soul. The struggle tested my commitment. At times I felt as though I'd lost sight of the vision entirely, only to emerge with a clearer sense than ever that I am precisely where I am meant to be at this moment.

ACTION STEPS—DARK NIGHT OF THE SOUL

Life challenges are inevitable. We don't talk about it, but few lives unfold without challenges. The same is true of careers. Most people I know, even those who have experienced success, have had many periods of uncertainty, ambiguity, and adversity.

What, then, can you do when you know there is going to be adversity but don't know what it will be or when? Sailing provides a powerful metaphor.

When sailing, we don't know what weather is coming or how other boats and ships are going to behave. There are no lines on the water to guide us once out of the harbor.

How, then, do we navigate with confidence?

First, the sailboat has a keel. The keel is the heavy metal fin that juts out of the bottom of the boat, giving the boat balance and strength.

Second, when we sail, we always have a destination, even if it is to enjoy the afternoon and return to port.

Third, the sailor has a general plan on how the boat is going to get from port to port. No sailboat leaves port with the crew thinking, *We'll just sail around for the rest of our lives.*

The same can be true for a work life. We wouldn't work for the rest of our lives without a keel to ground us, some destination to aim for, and a plan on how we are going to get there, along with reasonable provision for surprises along the way.

These simple assets are what prepare the crew, or in the case of your work life, *you,* for the uncertainties ahead. Here are a few simple steps you can take to prepare yourself for a future where life can change everything in ways that you can't prepare for!

1. What do you care about most in your work life? What truly,
    deeply, essentially matters to you? Clarity around what matters
    to you most is like a keel on the sailboat of your work life. It
    will keep you grounded and stable through the nastiest storm.

2. Where are you headed? What is your work life destination?
    Even a vague vision of the "sandy beach with palm trees" of
    your work life will prove enormously helpful when circum-
    stances change midstream. Your work life, like sailing around
    the world, will have waypoints, interim destinations to focus
    the next leg of the journey. What is your next waypoint on
    your work life voyage?

3. What is your plan for the next phase of the journey? You don't
    need specifics to get started, but given the prevailing condi-
    tions on the water, what course and direction do you want
    to follow? To arrive at your dream destination, do you need
    additional education? What skills might you need to develop?

4. As always, when making a major decision or charting a new
    course to a new destination, consult your guides. They can
    include your closest family members, friends, colleagues, or
    (better yet) someone with many years of experience who has
    nothing but your best interest at heart. Talk through what
    matters, where you want to be in five, ten, fifteen years, and
    how you believe you can get from here to there. Listen to their
    questions, not their advice, and decide for yourself the best
    adjustments to make. Like all good captains, pay attention to
    the changing conditions, on the water and in yourself, as you
    set out on your journey, making adjustments as you experi-
    ence changes along the way.

5. In Joseph Campbell's book *The Power of Myth*, he writes about
    the hero's (and heroine's) journey, where the dark night of the

soul is an essential part of the process of strengthening the hero/heroine for the journey ahead. It can feel depressing and disorienting when it feels as though all of our expectations have been dashed by unforeseen events. It is in these times that we remember what matters: keeping our eye on the destination and adjusting our plan as needed. Most importantly, it is during this time that we stay close to our guides, people who have navigated turbulent waters, and know that they are an essential part of a work life worth living. Picture yourself navigating your work life toward the distant shore, adjusting the path as conditions change on the waters that surround you. Add this "agile navigation" to your dream work life mural.

AI NOTE: AI can help you develop the vision of your future work life, including the course and direction you plan to follow to get there, always aware that changing conditions can cause you to navigate to a different heading on a moment's notice.

A WORK LIFE WORTH LIVING

My work life journey thus far has been marked by opportunity, calamity, faith, persistence, advancement, growth, adversity, pain, success, failure, joy, and sadness. I've shaped it, and I've been shaped by it. Thanks to enormous privilege, exceptional risk, passionate commitment, synchronous forces, and wise guidance, I've been granted an opportunity to do what I can to support others as they navigate the uncertain but eternally promising and hopeful waters ahead.

In a world with so much programming from schools to TV to social media and now AI, we can lose sight of what truly matters to us. The first step, and the step we can keep taking as our experience shapes us and the world changes around us, is to ask ourselves: What do I truly, deeply care about?

This is harder than it sounds. After each chapter, I've offered simple action steps that you can take on your own to help you navigate your way toward a more meaningful and fulfilling work life. Your work life will provide more than enough challenges to fuel your journey! And anticipating that you might want more help and that you might crave connection with others like yourself, we've created MeaningSphere. com, where you will find resources carefully curated to help you begin at the beginning, getting to know yourself and what matters to you about work.

Many people don't have access to experienced individuals who are trained in how to be a supportive guide. As members explore their beliefs and feelings about work, life, and what matters most to them, MeaningSphere guides offer a safe, confidential environment in which to support you as you navigate your journey.

In the late 1980s and early '90s when I was early in my career, few people were talking about the meaning of work. My friends and family weren't particularly interested in spending much time exploring these ideas, and neither were my peers—all good people absorbed in the myriad life and work challenges before them.

For many, I seemed like a hopeless idealist who wasn't willing to accept reality. It was a lonely journey, and as I look back, I could have worked harder to connect with others who were on a similar path. I'm not sure where I would have found them, but I know they were out there, somewhere.

To make it easier to connect, gain support, learn from, and help support others who know there must be more to work than simply collecting a paycheck, MeaningSphere offers the opportunity to join a community of individuals like yourself, people who want their work lives to mean more.

Going together is way better than going it alone. Not only do peers give us a sense of connection and belonging that can sustain us through our dark nights of the soul, but they also help propel us forward. As my friend and MeaningSphere cofounder Jory Tremblay reminds me, "If you want to go a short distance, go alone. If you want to go far, go together."

And like the many books that served as signposts for me along the road to the MeaningSphere, the platform offers practical tools to support you on your journey. Together with leading experts, researchers, and authors, we've curated a collection of experiences and forums that can help you explore, understand, and act toward the work life of your dreams, all in pragmatic, easy-to-apply, and self-guided methods made available at a price that almost anyone can afford.

And congratulations, if you have applied even 50 percent of the action steps offered in this book, you've now developed skills in self-reflection, consulting others, visioning, planning, and accessing artificial intelligence to turbocharge your natural intuitive and meaning-making abilities. Well done!

I hope my experiences, the lessons I learned from them, and the action steps I have offered you are helpful as you navigate toward your most meaningful work life. And for those interested in connecting with others on the path toward a more satisfying, rewarding, and ultimately fulfilling work life, MeaningSphere.com was created for you.

Your journey to a work life worth living awaits!

ONE BRICK AT A TIME

There is an undercurrent of unrest and disengagement in the workplace that's been building over the past decade. A May 2025 Gallup study indicates that 50 percent of US employees are either actively seeking or watching for new jobs—the highest since 2015.* And many of these people are wanting greater meaning, fulfillment, and alignment with personal values from their work.

There is no question that a movement toward more meaningful work is underway. But what is more meaningful work? Is it changing the work you do or changing how you see the work you are already doing or both?

For me, it was the last option—changing both things. On the surface, processing sales tax transactions could appear to be the most mundane and meaningless task on the planet. How would I ever feel satisfied, even fulfilled, by helping to build corporate transaction tax software? With the help of my mentor, who kept asking me, "What's

---

* "Regional Data Summary—State of the Global Workplace 2025," Gallup, 2025, https://www.gallup.com/workplace/697850/state-of-the-global-workplace-regional -data.aspx.

your purpose?" and "How do you intend to serve the greater whole?" it finally dawned on me.

The meaning wasn't in the product. It was in what the product did for people. Buy something online at Amazon? Only possible with transaction tax software. Enjoy a latte at Starbucks? Starbucks is breaking the law if they don't collect and remit the correct transaction taxes. Using AI to create the future of the world we live in? Only possible with the transaction tax software to meet legal requirements!

Our complex systems are composed of multiple parts. And those parts are so far removed from the finished product or service that we can lose sight of what we are creating when we put all the parts together.

In many ways, our individual work contributions are like individual bricks in a great bridge spanning generations. A single brick can't accomplish much on its own and is probably pretty lonely if it doesn't see itself as part of something larger than itself. But together, even a small number of bricks reinforce each other and create a foundation for a great bridge to the future.

It took millions of bricks to build the great bridges, roads, towns, and cities of the world we live in today. Together, they formed a great bridge from the agrarian world before the 1800s to the modern world we largely take for granted. Our parents, grandparents, and great-grandparents were among those millions. I had no idea I was part of building that great bridge until my mentor helped me see the reality that even the sales tax software was necessary to create roads, homes, social media sites, solar panels, and hospitals that seem to have appeared out of nowhere.

Whether you are aware of it or not, you have contributed to this march of progress as well. Whether it was babysitting, mowing the lawn, working at McDonalds, or any one of the millions of jobs people do, they all contribute in one way or another to creating and sustaining the world we live in today. Together, over the past century and through our individual contributions large and small, we have built a nation and a world, one brick at a time.

The world we have now, as imperfect as it is, is the world we built while we thought that all work was simply a way to make money. Imagine if we laid the next one hundred billion bricks with each of us understanding the bridge we are building, where that bridge leads us to, and what brick we are laying!

It starts with knowing what contribution we each want to make to that great bridge. What brick do you want to lay in its creation? Who do you want to work with to make your contribution more valuable? How do you want your work to impact your life? How do you want your life to impact your work? Who do you want to impact along the way, and what help can you provide others as others have helped you?

The answers to these questions can only come from within you. No bridge was built without every single brick it needed. Today, the brick I am contributing to the great bridge to our shared future is to create a space for anyone, anywhere to find out what their brick is meant to be and to ask us all to consider the ultimate question that only all of us can answer, together:

What is the meaning of this great bridge we are building, and where do we want it to take us?

ACKNOWLEDGMENTS

Living with a zealot who thinks business is a key to creating the future is no easy task, and my partner for life, Jenifer, has carried that load for nearly forty years. As I have reflected on the experiences that have shaped me and shaped the two of us, I cannot separate my evolution from hers. We are the two trees in Kahlil Gibran's famous poem:

> *Give your hearts, but not into each other's keeping.*
> *For only the hand of Life can contain your hearts.*
> *And stand together yet not too near together:*
> *For the pillars of the temple stand apart,*
> **And the oak tree and the cypress grow not**
> **in each other's shadow.**[*]

Thank you, my darling, for being the oak to my cypress on this glorious journey.

To our children, who have all expressed a wish that I had been there for them more, thank you for giving me your blessing, appreciating

---

[*] Kahlil Gibran, "On Marriage," in *The Prophet* (Kahlil Gibran, 1923).

that I was doing the best I could, and that it wasn't a lack of love for you but a passion to pay forward my good fortune that animated our time apart. Annie, Kyle, and Jake, thank you for your love, understanding, and unending support.

To Antoinette and Ray Westphal, my gratitude is endless. Rest in peace.

To my family of origin who shaped who I became as I entered the world of full-time work. I feel fortunate to have had two driven parents, seeking to live the American dream; two sisters who were my fellow travelers, living the highs and lows of family and family business; and a posse of aunts, uncles, cousins, and in-laws who together formed the cast of the stage play of my life. Out of respect for your privacy, I have not shared the myriad joys, sorrows, and lessons that you've shared with me and that we have learned together over the years. Perhaps you will see my efforts to share my good fortune with others as a reflection, in some small part, of my gratitude for what our family has made possible. Thank you.

To my colleagues at Vertex, especially the members of the leadership team during my tenure, and our earliest employees: Frank Contigiani, Tome' Lyda, Jon Riewe, Bill Boyer, Jim Restivo, Sue Baker, Jan Mehnert, Gerry Hurley, Ed Wallace, John Groves, Jack Ferraioli, John Viglione, David Destefano, Jim Krebs, Barb Dyson, Alex Smith, Steve Richard, David Henkin, and Jen Kurtz. I don't have words to thank you properly. We did it together, and I will be forever grateful. In addition to my colleagues within the company, I deeply appreciate the role of our seasoned and caring board of directors during my Vertex tenure. In addition to Terry and Rich, Ric Andersen, Kevin Robert, Rick Stamm, and Brian Nejmeh, thank you.

There are too many amazing clients and partners to thank everyone by name, and at the same time, I would be remiss to not share my deepest appreciation to Michael Davis, Bradley Gayton, Susan Davis, Pat Guerin, Albert Lee, and Conrad Young. Together you helped guide the company, and the industry, into the future. Thank you.

To the "vision delegates" who dared to aspire to and imagine potential beyond what any of us thought possible, thank you for your courage. Nick Fitzgerald, Brenda Johnson, Jill Nestor, Phill Siewerth, Beth Zygmunt, Diana Ravenelle, Michael Peterson, Dottie Friday, Pat Durr, Kathleen Matthews, Judith Kerry, Andy Hartlove, Barb Tornetta, Charlie Carroll, Robert Schoener, David Skarzynski, Heather McDevitt, Nancy Orlando, Chris Zangrilli, Tony Matayas, and Tome' Lyda. Somehow, we managed to create the future and make the difference, just like we dreamed we would!

To the hundreds of people at Vertex who contributed to shaping the future of modern tax processing, enabling businesses as vast as Apple, Amazon, Comcast, and Starbucks to move the world forward, please know that if I could have known each of you personally, I would have. Without you, there would have been no company, no customers, no partners, and no impact. We did it together, each and every one of us. To all of you, each and every one of you, please know this: I love you and wish you the work lives of your dreams. I am eternally grateful for our longtime colleagues now departed, Penny Vennerholm, Nancy Cooper, Nancy Jordan, Chris Kohl, and Shawn Green; rest in peace.

To my mentors and myriad advisors and professional counselors, I would have never been able to keep the wheels on the road without you. In addition to Jim Patton, Rich Teerlink, Terry Kyle, and Joseph Jaworski, all featured within the book, I want to particularly thank Avril Reed, Lynn McGregor, and Pamela Ramsden; together you helped me access resources I didn't know I had. I am forever grateful.

To Dr. Hadley Williams and David Dell, your vast experience and wise counsel helped shine a light on the road ahead, always helping me see around the corners. Hadley, your contributions to MeaningSphere breathed life into our shared dream for it. Thank you so very much.

To Dr. Steve Treat, Michael Blanche, and Dr. George James, thank you for helping me keep my head and heart clear.

To Gail Townsend, Sally Gore, and Dave Baldwin, your mentorship set me in the right direction at a pivotal moment, and Gail, you stayed an always present guide on my journey to this very day, sharing your wisdom with me and our MeaningSphere colleagues. Thank you so very much.

And to Jory B., Jim C., and Joe Q., thank you for showing me the way, one day at a time.

Dr. Fredricka Reisman, Don Huizenga, and Ira Brind, I am grateful for your mentorship and encouragement.

To my cofounders at MeaningSphere, Jory Tremblay, Keith Lewish, and again, Alex Smith, thank you. Together, we crafted a vision and strategy that is true to our values and our dream of a more satisfying and impactful world of work. Without you, this book and MeaningSphere are nothing. You have my undying gratitude.

To my MeaningSphere colleagues, thank you for taking this journey together. Without you, there is no MeaningSphere, nor would I have the invaluable lessons I have learned in trying to create an enterprise none of us has ever before witnessed. Your faith and contributions are endlessly appreciated. Your contributions and passion for our purpose have informed and inspired the lessons I have tried to share in these pages as well as in the web pages you have lovingly brought into being.

To Susan Taylor, Joseph's indispensable partner at Generon, contributor to his wonderful foreword, and "keeper of the flame" at MeaningSphere, I thank you.

To our leaders and special advisors to MeaningSphere, Karen

Singletary, Sheri Buergey, Britni Miller, Jon Sappey, Renee Souillard, Daria Torres, and Mario Musa, I thank you.

To our partners at the Map of Meaning Trust, Dr. Marjolein Lips-Wiersma, Lani Morris, and Celine McKeown, thank you for your groundbreaking and tireless work on behalf of working people everywhere.

To Bonnie Benjamin-Phariss and our Mosaic Board, thank you for building a foundation for independent, meaningful learning together.

To my COO, Ngaire Duncan, who keeps the good ship JRW Media on the right tack regardless of the conditions on the water. Thank you, Ngaire.

A shout out to our partners at Formative: Jon, Elizabeth, Brenna, and Anil.

To Betty Sue Flowers, who said, "Trust the truth, Jeff." I had no idea that I had met someone who was so much more than an "editor." Thank you, Betty Sue. I will do my best.

To Alex Smith, what can I say? We've spent a work life together, and every single day mattered. We aren't here without your tireless commitment to doing the right thing.

To Heather Stettler, whose fresh perspective added substantial depth and insight to the text in its final iterations. I appreciate the professionals of Greenleaf Book Group, an ideal partnership for this endeavor.

I owe a debt of gratitude to those who have gone before and to whose works and guidance I owe this book and MeaningSphere. To G. I. Gudjieff, John Bennett, Edward Matchett, Anthony Blake, C. Jung, Carl Rogers, Robert R. Carkhuff, Douglas McGregor, Stephen Covey, Peter Senge, Peter Schwartz, Gifford and Elizabeth Pinchot, Jon Katzenbach and Douglas K. Smith Jr., Joseph Jaworski, Meg Wheatley, Otto Scharmer, Daniel Pink, Simon Sinek, Martha Beck, Adam Grant, Brené Brown, Edward Wallace, Dr. George James, and most recently, Rick Rubin, I am grateful for the breadcrumbs you have laid on the path.

And finally, to Jim Patton, the work goes on. Rest in peace.

Jim and I enjoying a visit surrounded by his artwork, Greenville, Delaware, 2017

MEET THE EDITORS

BETTY SUE FLOWERS

Betty Sue is the former director of the Lyndon Baines Johnson Library and Museum and an emeritus professor of English at the University of Texas at Austin. She was the editor of Joseph Campbell's book *The Power of Myth* and acted as a consultant to the 1988 documentary series of the same name that featured interviews between Campbell and Bill Moyers. She also coauthored the book *Presence: Human Purpose and the Field of the Future* (2004) with Peter M. Senge, C. Otto Scharmer, and Joseph Jaworski. Flowers has had a career as a veteran practitioner of scenario planning (a strategic foresight method) for corporations, governments, and international organizations and recently authored *Scenarios: Crafting and Using Stories of the Future to Change the Present* (2026).

ALEX FORD SMITH

Alex has worked closely with Jeff for nearly four decades and is an award-winning journalist, public relations professional, brand executive, and business strategist. He is a cofounder of Jeff's latest venture, the MeaningSphere. Prior to that, he led the development of the brand, marketing communications, corporate communications, and government relations functions at Vertex, Inc. He was a member of Vertex's executive leadership team for fifteen years. Alex is the founder and president of Kairos Strategy LLC, an independent business advisory firm.

APPENDIX: RESOURCES

LIST OF RESOURCES NOTED IN THE TEXT

Tools for Self-Assessment

These tools are similar to FranklinCovey's multi-rater approach with peer, manager, and self-assessments for actionable insights.

- **Leadership Circle Profile (LCP):** Comprehensive 360-degree feedback on reactive and creative leadership styles, with detailed reports for coaching.

- **GLA360 by Marshall Goldsmith:** Assesses fifteen global leadership competencies, including qualitative feedback from Fortune 100 executives.

- **Hogan 360:** Combines personality assessments with 360 ratings to predict leadership derailers and strengths.

- **Korn Ferry 360:** Focuses on behavioral competencies with robust analytics for executive development.

- **STAR360feedback:** Offers self-debriefing reports, pulse surveys, and e-learning for ongoing team growth.

Meaningful Work

Marjolein Lips-Wiersma has primarily authored books on meaningful work and ethics, with her most notable being *The Map of Meaning: A Guide to Sustaining Our Humanity in the World of Work* (coauthored with Lani Morris, first published 2011 by Greenleaf Publishing) and its second edition, *The Map of Meaningful Work: A Practical Guide to Sustaining Our Humanity* (2017).

Dr. Sarah Wright, an associate professor of organizational behavior at the University of Canterbury, New Zealand, has published extensively on workplace loneliness, meaningful work, and leadership. She frequently collaborates with Marjolein Lips-Wiersma on these topics.

Key Joint Publications:

- Marjolein Lips-Wiersma and Sarah Wright, "Measuring the Meaning of Meaningful Work: Development and Validation of the Comprehensive Meaningful Work Scale (CMWS)," *Group & Organization Management* 37, no. 5 (2012): 655–85, https://psycnet.apa.org/doi/10.1177/1059601112461578.

- Marjolein Lips-Wiersma, Sarah Wright, and Bryan Dik, "Meaningful Work: Differences Among Blue-, Pink-, and White-Collar Occupations," *Career Development International* 21, no. 5 (2016): 534–51, DOI:10.1108/CDI-04-2016-0052.

- Marjolein Lips-Wiersma, Sarah Wright, and Jarrod M. Haar, "The Effect of Fairness, Responsible Leadership and Worthy Work on Multiple Dimensions of Meaningful Work," *Journal of Business Ethics* 161, no. 1 (2020): 1–18, DOI:10.1007/s10551-018-3967-2.

LIST OF BOOKS REFERRED TO IN THE TEXT (AND POSSIBLY OTHERS)

- Campbell, Joseph, *The Power of Myth* (Vintage, 1991).

- Covey, Stephen, *The 7 Habits of Highly Effective People: Powerful Lessons in Personal Change* (Simon & Schuster, 2004).

- Flowers, Betty Sue, *Scenarios: Crafting and Using Stories of the Future to Change the Present* (Bushe-Marshak Institute for Dialogic Organizational Development, 2026).

- Getz, Isaac and Laurent Marbacher, *The Caring Company: How to Shift Business and the Economy for Good* (Wiley, 2025).

- James, George, *I Give Myself Permission: Take Risks. Be Imperfect. Live Boldly.* (New Harbinger, 2026).

- Jaworski, Joseph, *Source: The Inner Path of Knowledge Creation* (Berrett-Koehler, 2012).

- Jaworski, Joseph, *Synchronicity: The Inner Path of Leadership*, 2nd ed. (Berrett-Koehler, 2011).

- Katzenbach, Jon R. and Douglas K. Smith, *The Wisdom of Teams: Creating the High-Performance Organization* (HBR Press, 2015).

- Kohn, Alfie, *Punished by Rewards: The Trouble with Gold Stars, Incentive Plans, A's, Praise, and Other Bribes*, 25th Anniversary ed. (HarperOne, 2018).

- Pink, Daniel H., *Drive: The Surprising Truth About What Motivates Us* (Riverhead, 2011).

- Senge, Peter M., *The Fifth Discipline: The Art & Practice of the Learning Organization* (Doubleday, 2006).

- Senge, Peter, C. Otto Scharmer, Joseph Jaworski, and Betty Sue Flowers, *Presence: Human Purpose and the Field of the Future* (Crown Currency, 2008).
- Teerlink, Rich and Lee Ozley, *More Than a Motorcycle: The Leadership Journey at Harley-Davidson* (Harvard Press, 2000).

MENTAL HEALTH RESOURCES

Free, confidential resources exist nationwide for personal challenges like mental health, stress, relationships, and financial issues, as well as professional ones such as workplace burnout or career transitions, including specialized support for alcoholism and addiction.

Immediate Crisis Support (Call/Text)

- **988 Suicide & Crisis Lifeline:**
  Call or text 988 (US & Canada) for confidential
  24/7 support in suicidal crisis or emotional distress.

- **Crisis Text Line:**
  Text HOME to 741741 to connect with
  a trained crisis counselor.

- **911:** For immediate, life-threatening emergencies; ask for an operator who has received crisis intervention training
  if possible.

- **Veterans Crisis Line:**
  Call 988 and press 1, text 838255, or chat online for
  military members, veterans, and their families.

Non-Crisis and Ongoing Support

- **NAMI (National Alliance on Mental Illness):**
  (1-800-950-6264) Offers local support, education,
  and advocacy.

- **HelpLine:**
  1-800-950-NAMI (6264) or text NAMI to 62640.

- **Mental Health America:**
  Provides resources, including warm lines for
  non-crisis support.

- **The Trevor Project:**
  Crisis intervention and suicide prevention for
  LGBTQ young people (text START to 678-678).

- **FindTreatment.gov:**
  Directory for mental health and substance use
  treatment providers.

Tips for Emergencies

- If you call 911, state that it is a psychiatric emergency
  and request a crisis-trained officer if available.

- Warm lines are available for non-crisis support
  when you just need someone to talk to.

Addiction and Substance Use Helplines

These 24/7 services offer anonymous referrals, crisis support, and
treatment locators without requiring personal details.

- **SAMHSA National Helpline:**
  1-800-662-HELP (4357) for mental health, substance use,
  and co-occurring disorders; available in English/Spanish.

- **NIAAA Alcohol Treatment Navigator:**
  Online tool for evidence-based alcohol treatment matching.

- **National Drug Helpline:**
  1-844-289-0879 for addiction support and referrals.

Mutual Support Groups for Addiction

Peer-led meetings emphasize anonymity and are free for those experiencing alcoholism, drug use, or behavioral addictions.

- **Alcoholics Anonymous (AA):**
  In-person/online meetings; app available; 212-870-3400.

- **Narcotics Anonymous (NA):**
  Similar 12-step program for all drugs.

- **SMART Recovery:**
  Science-based, non-12-step meetings; 440-951-5357.

- **LifeRing and Women for Sobriety:**
  Secular options tailored to needs; 800-811-4142
  or 215-536-8026.

- **Adult Children of Alcoholics (ACA):**
  adultchildren.org; 12-step approach to self-development
  for family and friends impacted by alcoholism
  and addiction; (310) 534-1815.

Workplace and Professional Resources

- Employee Assistance Programs (EAPs) via employers
  provide confidential counseling for job stress, alcoholism,
  or performance issues; federal workers can access
  OPM guidance.

- For broader professional challenges, use SAMHSA's
  locator or NIAAA professional associations like American
  Psychological Association (1-800-374-2721).